Inspirations From
Northern Ireland
Edited by Claire Tupholme

 Young**Writers**

First published in Great Britain in 2007 by:
Young Writers
Remus House
Coltsfoot Drive
Peterborough
PE2 9JX
Telephone: 01733 890066
Website: www.youngwriters.co.uk

SB ISBN 978-1 84431 241 2

Foreword

Young Writers was established in 1991 and has been passionately devoted to the promotion of reading and writing in children and young adults ever since. The quest continues today. Young Writers remains as committed to the nurturing of poetic and literary talent as ever.

This year's Young Writers competition has proven as vibrant and dynamic as ever and we are delighted to present a showcase of the best poetry from across the UK and in some cases overseas. Each poem has been selected from a wealth of *Little Laureates* entries before ultimately being published in this, our sixteenth primary school poetry series.

Once again, we have been supremely impressed by the overall quality of the entries we have received. The imagination, energy and creativity which has gone into each young writer's entry made choosing the poems a challenging and often difficult but ultimately hugely rewarding task - the general high standard of the work submitted ensured this opportunity to bring their poetry to a larger appreciative audience.

We sincerely hope you are pleased with this final collection and that you will enjoy *Little Laureates Inspirations From Northern Ireland* for many years to come.

Contents

Síoneen McMahon (8)	71
Eryn Murphy (9)	71
Gabrielle Fox (9)	72
Kelly McMahon (9)	72
Carolyn Fitzpatrick (9)	73
Padraig Renaghan (8)	73
Ciara Mallon (9)	74
Rebecca McNaughton (7)	74
James Murray (9)	74
Marie-Claire Burke (9)	75
Shane Donnelly (9)	75
Shannon McGuigan (9)	75
Ellen Hamilton (8)	76
Gareth Whyte (9)	76
Alice Lennon (8)	77
Bernice Conlon (9)	77
Pauric McNaughton (9)	78
Emma Mone (8)	78
Bronagh Downey	79
Keelin Boyd (9)	79
Pearse Lennon (8)	79
Emma Rice (10)	80
Catherine Anne Nugent (8)	80
Dína Heavin (9)	81
Eimear McCarthy (8)	81
Sinead McKee (10)	82
Orla Breen (10)	82
Martina McNally (10)	83
Jennifer Lynch (9)	83
Michael McGrane (10)	84
Hannah Finnegan (10)	84

St Brendan's Primary School, Craigavon

Christine Hart (10)	85
Orla Lamph (10)	85
Christopher Fitzsimmons (10)	85
Rhiannon Haughian (10)	86
Alana Hughes (10)	86
Luke Devlin (9)	86
Ellie McKeagney (9)	87

St Joseph's Primary School, Caledon

Caolan Gormley (10)	87
Louise Carey (9)	87
Erin McCausland (9)	88
Ciaran Shevlin (9)	88
Clare McKenna (11)	88
Kerry Hornsey (10)	89
Kelli Loughran (11)	89
Catherine O'Gorman (10)	90
Kevin Magnone (11)	90
Caoimhe Hughes (11)	90
Luke Sherry (9)	91
Patrick McKenna (9)	91
Siobhan Wray (11)	91
Sarah-Louise Hughes (10)	92

St Mary's Primary School, Craigavon

Aaron Doherty (9)	92
Miamph Hanlon (10)	93
Josh Kane (9)	93
Caoimhe Bunting (10)	94
Cormac Lavery (9)	94
PJ McGarrity (10)	95
Tiernan Kane-Cavanagh (9)	95
Rebecca Harbinson (9)	96
Caolan Farr (10)	97
Aaron Mooney (10)	98
Molly Lavery (9)	99
Aoife McGuinness (9)	100
Rebekah Clenaghan (9)	101
Monica McCavigan (9)	101
Eimhear Bunting (10)	102
Caoimhe Holden (9)	102
Eunan Walsh (9)	103
Kieran Lavery (10)	103
Holleah McNally (10)	104
Leeanne Nelson (9)	104
Lisa Bunting (9)	105
Natasha Doone (9)	105
Chloe Doone (9)	106
Conaire Lavery (10)	106

St Patrick's Primary School, Downpatrick

Sean Murphy (11)	107
Daniel Kelly (11)	107
Manus Kelly (11)	108
Conor Mullan (11)	108
Mark Robinson (11)	109
Matthew Campbell (11)	109
Ryan Kearney (11)	110
Johnny Collins (11)	110
Nathan Oakes (11)	111
Jamie Fitzpatrick (11)	111
Ryan Vaughan (11)	112
Gareth Robinson (11)	113
Paul Martin (11)	114
Dylan Graham (10)	115
Jonathan Deeny (11)	116
Adam Kerr	116
Joel McConvey (11)	117
Christopher McKenna (10)	117

St Teresa's Primary School, Mountnorris

Michael McQuaide (11)	118
Hannah Feenan (11)	118
Anastasia Ni Riabhaigh (10)	119
Margaret McQuaide (9)	119
Julie McSherry (11)	120
Emma Vint (10)	120
Lee Carr	121
Ryan McSherry (8)	121
Niamh Kelly (10)	122
Tracey McSherry (11)	122
Shania Ruddy (8)	123

The Irish Society's Primary School, Coleraine

Mahnoor Tughral (11)	123
Danni Millar (11)	124
Sarah Sim (11)	124
Hayley Gibson (11)	125
Claire Cooper (11)	126

The Poems

The Big Round Earth

The Earth is a huge coin
Coloured in gold or silver
The Earth is a very big face
Painted in green or blue
The Earth is someone's eye
A blue or green eye
The Earth is a massive circle
That you can use in school
The Earth is a very big football
That is green and blue.

Amy Robinson (9)
Aughnacloy Primary School, Aughnacloy

Little Stars In The Sky

Little stars shine at night
Little stars twinkle at night
You see the stars glow
You see the stars flow
The stars are bright yellow
A bright yellow star
Rises in the night.

Lucy Marshall (9)
Aughnacloy Primary School, Aughnacloy

Happiness

Happiness smells like chilli
Happiness feels like a pebble
Happiness looks like a phoenix rising from the ashes
Happiness tastes like chilli sauce
Happiness is life.

Dylan Kyle (8)
Aughnacloy Primary School, Aughnacloy

Little Star

Little star, little star
You shine at night
And always so bright
I look up when I am in the car
Little star, little star.

Little star, little star
So like gold
I was told
So far away
Can't wait to see you some day
Little star, little star.

Hayley Marshall (9)
Aughnacloy Primary School, Aughnacloy

My Cat

Greedy and loving
Cute and cuddly
Big and fast
Black and white
Furry and loveable
His name is Lucky.

Lee Graham (8)
Aughnacloy Primary School, Aughnacloy

The Little Horse

My horse is small
He has little legs
But he runs fast
People think Brownie is kind
But I think he is really everything!

Rachel Vennard (8)
Aughnacloy Primary School, Aughnacloy

My Little Kitten

My little kitten is cute,
She is a little mute,
My little kitten is so good you know,
She will tidy up in the snow,
She is so fast and lovely,
Small, yet strong you know,
But now she's getting bigger,
Into a big, fat cat,
And a little bit black.

Laura Donaldson (8)
Aughnacloy Primary School, Aughnacloy

Chelsea FC

C helsea Football Club
H ave scored a lot of goals
E ven when they played
L ampard scored and rolled
S amsung Mobile sponsors them
E very week they practise
A nd hope that they will win

F or every cup they get, they'll be the
C hampions.

Chelsea Gillis (8)
Aughnacloy Primary School, Aughnacloy

My Dog Holly

Greedy and speedy
Helpful and playful
Loveable and beautiful
And she is a rascal.

Daniel Morrow (9)
Aughnacloy Primary School, Aughnacloy

The Golden Dog

G old is a lovely colour for a dog to be
O dd she was, she jumped on your arm
L oveable, she was careful and sweet
D o you think she was cute? Yes, she was so, so cute
'E at your dinner,' I said and she did
N aughty sometimes but I miss her so.

Rebekah Adams (8)
Aughnacloy Primary School, Aughnacloy

My Dog

J is for jog, to run slowly
A is for alone without any others
C is for cat, a furry animal
K is for kennel, a hut for my dog.

Arlene Gibson (9)
Aughnacloy Primary School, Aughnacloy

Silence/Noise

Silence:

Silence is what you hear when you're alone,
Silence goes in your ear when noise is postponed.
Some people like silence and some do not,
But as for me, silence is good and noise is not.

Noise:

Noise is a good thing when you're having a party,
Noise is fun when you are feeling lively.
Some people like noise and some people do not,
But as for me, noise is good and silence is not.

Robert McCullough (11)
Benburb Primary School, Benburb

Anger

Anger tastes like fire
Anger tastes like ashes of the dead

Anger looks like lava from a volcano

Anger feels like the Devil

Anger reminds me of Hell.

Andrew Irwin (10)
Benburb Primary School, Benburb

Fun

Fun sounds like laughter,
It tastes like millions of toys,
Although it smells like love and caring,
It feels like home,
It reminds me of all the things I have in my life.

Gillian Sloane (11)
Benburb Primary School, Benburb

Hunger

Hunger tastes like freshly baked pizza.
Hunger smells like crispy bacon.
Hunger looks like chips a-taken.
Hunger feels like a rumbling tum.
Hungry is a terrible way to be.

Jonathan Ewing (10)
Benburb Primary School, Benburb

My Puppy Shadow

My faithful friend is my puppy Shadow
He bounces up when I bend low
To allow him to lick my face
Before I can take another pace.

His coat is black and white
With two large spots placed just right
On the centre of his broad back
A real beauty with nothing to lack.

His long soft ears are as soft as silk
His favourite drink is warm milk
His sympathetic eyes are soft brown
A special puppy who deserves a crown.

Sharon Johnston (10)
Benburb Primary School, Benburb

Summer

Summer is here,
It's that time of year,
Where you splash in the sea,
Right up to your knee.

No more homework to do,
Just trips to the zoo.
Bicycles race around the park,
We can stay out until dark!

We play on our swings,
Lots of ice cream and things.
Lazy days go by,
Oh summer, don't fly!

Jessica Pogue (10)
Benburb Primary School, Benburb

My Cat

My cat snowball is the softest thing I've ever felt.
She is a one-year-old and lots of fun,
She is like a shining star,
She is so cute with her nice white fur,
We nearly lost her in the snow.

When we pet her silky fur it is so soft,
She loves to play with my table tennis ball,
She fights with Sandy the dog,
The fur on her back stands tall.

She really is a special cat to all of us,
We are her family now,
She is so happy here,
I wish I had her a long time ago.

David Barr (9)
Bushvalley Primary School, Stranocum

My Dog

My dog's name is Holly,
It could have been Molly.
Her collar is as shiny as a diamond ring
From my uncle's jewellers.
She eats like a messy pig
And smells like one too, without shampoo.
Her strong bark is like a lion's roar,
She has brown fur like a bunny's tail.
When she jumps in the air,
I think to myself, *wow!*
When I brush her silk coat,
It gleams in the sun
And that is why I love her so much.

Rebecca Whyte (10)
Bushvalley Primary School, Stranocum

The Chocolate Shetland

The chocolate Shetland
At the side of the road
Like a silky black unicorn
In Shetland's clothes.

He has the heart of a lion
And a scruffy mane,
He drives some people so insane
As he howls at the moon like a wise old wolf.

When I reach out
And touch his silky fur,
I much prefer him
To a hot-water bottle.

Even though I moan and cry in pain,
As he is behind a tall silver fence in chains,
He is a captured prisoner there,
Held by the Master of Mean.

Alexandra Cameron (11)
Bushvalley Primary School, Stranocum

Pepsi

He's soft with a hard, shiny nose.
That nose is cold,
He's very old.
He's rather fat
And his eyes are so small.
After all this time
His fur is black.
He's my favourite toy,
I love him.

Rachel McBride (9)
Bushvalley Primary School, Stranocum

Young Writers - Little Laureates Inspirations From Northern Ireland

My Tricycle

My old tricycle, it was red like a fox,
Fast as lightning.
When I was on it,
It was like there was no tomorrow.
When I was on it,
It squeaked like a mouse.

It had a bell on it
With a bucket at the back.
I thought that it was the most precious thing
In the whole wide world.

When I broke my treasured tricycle,
I knew I would never
Have one like that again.

Danielle McMullan (11)
Bushvalley Primary School, Stranocum

My Little Brother

My little brother can be
As sweet as Granny's chocolate cake.

My little brother can be
As sneaky as a spy.

My little brother can be
As annoying as a bug -
He creeps into my room and roars
Boo!
And I jump as high as a soaring rocket.

Would you like a little brother?

Saffron Hoy (10)
Bushvalley Primary School, Stranocum

Tractor

My wee small tractor,
In the grass it was camouflaged,
We carted silage,
With low mileage.
We scraped a cow dropping,
Without mopping it.
I made a farm from sticks and stones,
Thank goodness I didn't break any bones.
I got taller
And not any smaller,
And soon I was a tree,
And it was a pebble.
I couldn't ride it,
I could only hide it,
Shut away from the world forever.

Peter Dunlop (11)
Bushvalley Primary School, Stranocum

My House

My house is tall and long like a giraffe.
It's black and white like a galloping zebra.
When I walk on the wooden floors,
It sounds like a horse in a concrete stable.

I think my house is much nicer than the others,
With a gleaming red door,
Shining like glossy cherries.
My house isn't just a building,
It's my home.

Stacey Brown (9)
Bushvalley Primary School, Stranocum

My Granny's Handbag

My granny's handbag was
Dark black and cream,
It was made with scaly leather,
A long tassel hung down one side like a
Long cream snake slithering down a slide.

When the tassels hit the bag it made a
Click-clack sound
Like a horse trotting up the road.

It smelt like a whole shop of leather,
But I didn't mind.
The very first time I saw it I thought to myself,
I hope I own a bag like that one day!

Jodie McBride (11)
Bushvalley Primary School, Stranocum

My Brother And Our Car

My fearless brother got into the car,
He was only three or four,
Then quickly he turned the key,
Laughing like a hyena.

He started towards the sharp pointed fence,
Like a train crossing a tightrope,
Zooming for the prickly green hedge,
While I fearfully peeped over the window ledge.

Mum stopped the car,
It's a good thing it didn't go that far.

Clare McGurk (10)
Bushvalley Primary School, Stranocum

My Dog

My dog, Tara, she's as funny as a clown,
Always chasing her tail like a merry-go-round.
Looks like a rabbit on the run,
Likes to chill out in the sun.
Tara, also known as Lady,
Always rolling over just like a baby.
Cheers you up when you're feeling down,
You'll never see her make us frown.
With her fur as soft as silk,
She's like a good old drink of water,
Gets treated like a human daughter!
Lady hates my granny's cats,
Probably thinks they're wicked old bats.
But still we love her through and through,
Even when she does a . . .
. . . Well, you know what I mean!

Matthew Christie (10)
Bushvalley Primary School, Stranocum

My Quad

My little quad was golden yellow,
Like a lion's mane.
When I went whooshing through the fields,
I thought I was on an aeroplane.
My dad watched and made us tracks,
But then sadly my little quad passed away.
We took him to the doctor to see what he could do,
He only spluttered one more time.
I said goodbye and he was gone.
I wish I had him back again.

Mark Henry (11)
Bushvalley Primary School, Stranocum

Massey Ferguson

My grandad's red Massey Ferguson
Shone brightly in the sun,
When it was on the road
It looked like a fox
Stalking and ambushing its prey.
It always smelt of smoke
From the tall, black exhaust.
When he took me for rides,
I thought I was in an aeroplane instead of a tractor
Because I was up so high.
When he started it up,
It sounded like a snoring lion in the sun.
Why don't they make tractors like that anymore?

Peter Crowe (11)
Bushvalley Primary School, Stranocum

My Bro's F1 Car

When I was a child
My brother had an F1 car.
It gleamed in the sun
It was as red as a cherry on a bun.
When you touched it
It was as hard as the road,
But at that time
I was slithering about like a toad.
When it sat in the sun for a while,
It smelt like plastic -
Oh boy! It was fantastic!

Terry-Lee Horner (11)
Bushvalley Primary School, Stranocum

My Mum's High Heels

Clipping and clopping about
Like a horse in the stable,
Trying to walk in high heels
If I was able.

They were red and shiny
Just like Rudolph's nose,
I wore my mum's dress
That swayed and flowed.

I tripped and fell to the ground
Like a leaf on a windy day,
Then I said to myself
'How does Mum dress that way?'

Kelly McLean (11)
Bushvalley Primary School, Stranocum

My Granny's Sugar Sandwiches

My granny's sugar sandwiches
Were as tasty as a cool drink on a hot, sunny day.
She would make them secretly without telling my mum,
We would feast on them like lions eating their prey.
Then when Mummy came we hid them from her,
Like secret agents do.
I had tasted nothing like it before
And the way I have described it,
I now want to eat some more.
Don't you?

Hannah Johnston (11)
Bushvalley Primary School, Stranocum

Playing Dress-Up

My mum's favourite lipstick
Is a deep, dark red.
I loved to smudge it on my
Lips, cheeks and forehead.

I used it while playing dress-up
With my sister,
Even though Mum's shoes
Gave me a blister.

This is my favourite memory,
The best of all,
For it's a memory
From when I was small.

Seón Simpson (11)
Bushvalley Primary School, Stranocum

My Daddy's Boots

My daddy's boots are as black as coal,
Inside and out.
When I walked in them,
They made a thudding sound,
Like an elephant would.
They were hard and smooth as a pebble
You would find on a beach.
The pattern on the bottom of the shoes
Was like jelly cubes.
Inside it was as smooth as the silk
You would find on your dress.
That is why I like my daddy's boots.

Ellen Walker (11)
Bushvalley Primary School, Stranocum

My Granda's Tractor

My granda has a tractor
That's as red as a fox
Slinking in the shadows.
It's as clean as a whistle,
For a tractor anyway.
When he turns the key,
The engine roars like a tiger
Hunting his prey.

When my granda changed gear,
There was a loud creak,
Like a squeaky door.
If we came to a bump,
The seats would bounce
Like kangaroos.

The big back wheels
Were as tough as old boots
And the paintwork was as smooth
As an expensive silk dress.

It could probably lift anything
Because it's as strong as an elephant.
I always sat on my special seat
In my granda's old International.
Why did I love it so much?

Amy McIlhatton (11)
Bushvalley Primary School, Stranocum

My Uncle's Massey

My uncle's Massey
With glimmering
Bright colours
When he brought it out
Of the shed there
Was a flurry of
Light and sound.
The seat was as
Soft as pillows
But I can't say it had
Suspension though.
The fumes
Filled the air with a
Smoky fragrance.
But sadly it's gone now
I'll never see it again.
Why don't they make tractors
That way anymore?

Adam Montgomery (11)
Bushvalley Primary School, Stranocum

Spring

Easter's here, let's celebrate!
Fresh new life is everywhere,
Flowers are blooming,
Eggs are hatching and
Jesus has risen!
All around birds are singing,
Bunnies are bouncing
And hopping with glee,
Quack, quack say the ducklings,
Spring is great!

Emily Richardson (9)
Carnaghts Primary School, Shankbridge

Holidays

Slippery fish jumping out of water,
Families relaxing by the pool,
Lazily lying and sunbathing too!
Gentle breezes coming from the north,
Snazzy restaurants with tasty food,
Beach balls bouncing here and there!
Hot, sandy beaches,
All holidays are good fun!

Emma McKay (9)
Carnaghts Primary School, Shankbridge

Spring

Lambs bumping into each other
Daffodils bloom, all shapes and sizes
Sheep running and jumping
Fresh new life is everywhere
High in the sky, the birds fly
Girls and boys play Frisbee games
I am happy spring is here
Bunnies bouncing and hopping with glee.

Rebecca Duff (9)
Carnaghts Primary School, Shankbridge

Spring

Easter's here, come celebrate!
Hallelujah, Jesus has arisen.
Terrific long and sunny days.
Little chicks hide shyly under Mother's wing.
Bluebells make a purple carpet.
Fresh new life is everywhere.
I love spring!

Andrew Hogg (9)
Carnaghts Primary School, Shankbridge

Spring

Ducks are playing in the pond
Fresh life is everywhere
Easter's here, come celebrate
Now is the springtime
All around birds are singing
High in the sky birds fly
People walking through the park
Boys and girls playing together.

Marshall Gillan (9)
Carnaghts Primary School, Shankbridge

Spring

Spring is here, what a joy it brings
Seedlings open, what a sight to see
Lambs are skipping and hopping all around
Blossoms pink, white or cream, any colour you can pick
High above we see birds singing
Easter eggs are so yummy and tasty
Bunnies bouncing and hopping with glee
Fresh new life is everywhere.

Lesley-Anne Doran (9)
Carnaghts Primary School, Shankbridge

Spring

Hooray! Jesus is alive.
Fresh new life everywhere.
Creation has broken into life.
Bunnies hopping with glee.
Daffodils bloom, all shapes and sizes.
Yellow chicks cheeping happily.
Quacking ducklings everywhere.
Easter's here! Come celebrate!

Jacqueline Mulholland (9)
Carnaghts Primary School, Shankbridge

Holidays

I'm away at last on my holiday
Fun is happening in the pool
Buckets and spades are going speedily
Every child is catching crabs
Dripping ice cream all over the children
Come lie with me lazily
Great sunny weather is here.

Laura Marshall (9)
Carnaghts Primary School, Shankbridge

Spring

Eggs hatching with happy chicks
High in the sky birds fly
Jesus rose again for us
Lambs jumping and skipping happily
Quacking ducks everywhere
Rabbits' holes dug here and there
Seedlings grow happily
Tulips bloom all around
White, woolly lambs being born.

Kathryn Francey (9)
Carnaghts Primary School, Shankbridge

Fear

It reminds me of death
It looks like caskets
Fear is red like blood
It tastes like dead people
It sounds like killings
It feels like sadness.

Jamie Wiseman (10)
Drumgor Primary School, Drumgor

Laughter

It looks like happiness
It reminds me of school
It feels like a feather on your foot
It smells like Lynx
It tastes like chocolate
It sounds like enjoyment
It is white and black like a football.

Benjamin Lewis (10)
Drumgor Primary School, Drumgor

Darkness

Darkness is black, like night
It smells like candles
It reminds me of sleeping
It sounds like singing
It tastes like fumes
It feels like air
It looks like anything.

Andrew Ruddell (10)
Drumgor Primary School, Drumgor

Sadness

It feels like water
It sounds like a tap dripping
It smells like dead roses
It reminds me of my granny
It tastes like vinegar
Sadness is blue, like teardrops.

Rebecca Lyness (9)
Drumgor Primary School, Drumgor

Anger

It sounds like heat
It reminds me of shouting
It feels like dead roses
It smells like vinegar
Anger is black, like a rock
It looks like red roses
It tastes like cabbage.

Reese Thompson (10)
Drumgor Primary School, Drumgor

Love

Love is red, like roses
It tastes like sweets
It reminds me of hearts
It looks like hearts
It sounds like happiness
It smells like flowers
It feels like love.

Jordan Smylie (10)
Drumgor Primary School, Drumgor

Fear

It feels like water
It looks like dead flowers
It reminds me of my nanny
It tastes like salt
It sounds like water from a tap
It smells like flowers.

Alysha Cousins (9)
Drumgor Primary School, Drumgor

Darkness

It feels like rocks
It sounds like screams
It reminds me of death
It looks like a shadow
It smells like smoke
It is black, like the night sky
It tastes like bad food.

Mia Robinson (10)
Drumgor Primary School, Drumgor

Silence

It reminds me of people being quiet
It feels like I am in a wood at night
It looks like the weather
It reminds me of sleeping
It tastes like an orange
It sounds like nothing
Silence is blue like the sky.

Kieran Donaghy (9)
Drumgor Primary School, Drumgor

Spring

Spring comes with children humming
Spring comes with sheep bleating
Spring comes with chicks cheeping
Spring comes with flowers blooming
Spring comes with tadpoles swimming
Spring comes with trees budding
Spring comes with birds tweeting
Spring comes with the wind whistling
Spring comes with fruit growing.

Laura Stewart (9)
Fair Hill Primary School, Dromara

I Went Back

I went back after a cold
And nothing was the same
They had learnt a new game
Even a new girl came
And had a pink school bag
And had a name tag
We got a new swing
And my friend got a ring
My best friend's colour is now pink
And now we write with ink
We are learning about flint
So my friend gave me a hint
They planted a tulip
My cold is nearly gone
I got to go on a trip
And got to keep the tulip.

Hayley Martin (9)
Fair Hill Primary School, Dromara

Jump Or Jiggle?

Frogs hop
Horses clop

Seagulls glide
Mice hide

Snakes wiggle
Worms jiggle

Grasshoppers jump
Caterpillars hump

Kittens bounce
Lions pounce

But I walk.

Lee Hamilton (9)
Fair Hill Primary School, Dromara

Summer

Summer comes
  With water splashing
Summer comes
  With people shivering
Summer comes
  With the ice cream van singing
Summer comes
  With bees stinging
Summer comes
  With the sun blinding
Summer comes
  With adults surfing
Summer comes
  With skin burning
Summer comes
  With flowers blooming.

Ryan Corbett (9)
Fair Hill Primary School, Dromara

Easter Comes

Easter comes
  With the eggs rattling
Easter comes
  With the bunny returning
Easter comes
  With a holiday coming
Easter comes
  With eggs rolling
Easter comes
  With flowers blooming
Easter comes
  With money giving.

Matthew Cooper (8)
Fair Hill Primary School, Dromara

Animal Movements

Lions roar
Larks soar

Tigers eat
Sheep bleat

Eagles glide
Snakes slide

Spiders creep
Mice peep

Cats lick
Birds pick

Foxes shoo
Cows moo

Monkeys jump
Elephants thump

Leopards stalk
But I walk.

Thomas Peters (9)
Fair Hill Primary School, Dromara

Summer

Summer comes
With school closing

Summer comes
With people smiling

Summer comes
With flowers blooming

Summer comes
With farmers bailing

Summer comes
With holidays starting

Summer comes
With people swimming

Summer comes
With having fun

Summer comes
With being happy.

Nicole Hamilton (9)
Fair Hill Primary School, Dromara

Christmas

Christmas comes
    With church bells ringing loudly
Christmas comes
    With children singing sweetly
Christmas comes
    With presents sitting beautifully
Christmas comes
    With lights flickering quickly
Christmas comes
    With the organ playing noisily
Christmas comes
    With toast-saying happily
Christmas comes
    With the turkey cooking nicely
Christmas comes
    With children snowman-making carefully
Christmas comes
    With cracker-pulling strongly
Christmas comes
    With snow falling heavily
Christmas comes
    With robins whistling peacefully
Christmas comes
    With tinsel shining brightly.

Adam Rodgers (9)
Fair Hill Primary School, Dromara

I Went Back

I went back after chickenpox
And nothing was the same.
We had new locks
And some new clocks.
A brand new bench which is blue,
Which we had to glue.
The teachers all drank coffee
And our treat was toffee.
Kenny had a magic thread,
For dinner I had garlic bread.
We had a new teacher to teach
And I missed a trip to the beach.
Bryan learnt to do an army crawl
And Andrew had a bad fall.
We got a brand new door
And a free floor.
We had a new school rabbit
And I had a bad habit.
I had missed out on a lot
But on Tuesday I caught up.
I got rid of the chickenpox
And I finished my project about the slugs in a box.
I got the rabbit till summer.

Andrew Rowan (9)
Fair Hill Primary School, Dromara

Christmas

Christmas comes
  With the choir singing
Christmas comes
  With my dad whistling
Christmas comes
  With my dog barking
Christmas comes
  With bells ringing
Christmas comes
  With Santa arriving
Christmas comes
  With reindeer flying
Christmas comes
  With presents coming
Christmas comes
  With snow falling
Christmas ends
  With children playing.

Jordan Rowan (9)
Fair Hill Primary School, Dromara

Summer

Summer comes
  With flowers blooming
Summer comes
  With children playing
Summer comes
  With birds singing
Summer comes
  With children swimming
Summer comes
  With people surfing
Summer comes
  With beach partying
Summer comes
  With bees buzzing
Summer comes
  With park climbing
Summer comes
  With holidays from school beginning.

Lauren Carlisle (9)
Fair Hill Primary School, Dromara

My Birthday

My birthday comes
    With invites wrinkling
My birthday comes
    With present shaking
My birthday comes
    With bouncy castle puffing
My birthday comes
    With face painting
My birthday comes
    With music singing
My birthday comes
    With decorations swinging
My birthday comes
    With cake munching
My birthday comes
    With party bags rustling.

Stuart Rankin (8)
Fair Hill Primary School, Dromara

This Christmas Time

C is for carols we sing at Christmas
H is for the ham we have at Christmas
R is for Rudolph who has a shiny nose
I is for ice that is on the ground
S is for snow we play in
T is for turkey that we eat
M is for the manger that the Lord Jesus lay in
A is for the Advent calendar we open every day
S is for the stockings we hang up on Christmas Eve.

Cameron Peel (8)
Fair Hill Primary School, Dromara

Afternoon

Afternoon comes
   With three dogs barking disturbingly
Afternoon comes
   With children playing happily
Afternoon comes
   With the school bell ringing loudly
Afternoon comes
   With children running on the pitch shouting joyfully
Afternoon comes
   With boys kicking playfully
Afternoon comes
   With homework books slamming cheerfully
Afternoon comes
   With birds singing sweetly
Afternoon comes
   With children talking, including me!

Victoria Reain (9)
Fair Hill Primary School, Dromara

Christmas Has Come To Town

C is for Christmas carols that fill my heart with cheer
H is for how I love this time of year
R is for Rudolph who guides the sleigh
 I is for inn where Mary and Joseph decided to stay
S is for the joy of the season I have found
T is for tinsel which on the tree we wrap around
M is for mistletoe where you get a kiss
A is for Advent and the chocolate we wouldn't miss
S is for shopping which lots of people do.

Jill Copes (9)
Fair Hill Primary School, Dromara

Summer

Summer comes
    With farmers lambing
Summer comes
    With holidays flying
Summer comes
    With children playing
Summer comes
    With beaches filling
Summer comes
    With birds cheeping
Summer comes
    With people swimming
Summer comes
    With parents laughing
Summer comes
    With flowers blooming.

Thomas Megarry (9)
Fair Hill Primary School, Dromara

How Animals Move

Rabbits hop
Frogs plop

Snakes wiggle
Worms jiggle

Horses jump
Elephants stomp

Mice squeak
Foxes sneak

Lions pounce
Lambs bounce

'Seagulls glide
Penguins slide.

Lauren Henry (9)
Fair Hill Primary School, Dromara

Young Writers - Little Laureates Inspirations From Northern Ireland

Summer

Summer comes
    With the sun blazing
Summer comes
    With the beaches filling
Summer comes
    With bees stinging
Summer comes
    With flowers blooming
Summer comes
    With birds singing
Summer comes
    With children playing
Summer comes
    With me shopping
Summer comes
    With bodies tanning
Summer comes
    With sunbathing
Summer comes
    With people talking
And that's me!

Laura Redmond (9)
Fair Hill Primary School, Dromara

Hallowe'en Comes

Hallowe'en comes
　　With fireworks sparkling
Hallowe'en comes
　　With people hiding
Hallowe'en comes
　　With people scaring
Hallowe'en comes
　　With children dressing
Hallowe'en comes
　　With dogs barking
Hallowe'en comes
　　With children shivering
Hallowe'en comes
　　With people celebrating
Hallowe'en comes
　　With houses creaking
Hallowe'en comes
　　With vampires drinking
Hallowe'en comes
　　With me relaxing.

Andrew Knox (9)
Fair Hill Primary School, Dromara

Evening

Evening comes
    With saucepans sizzling
Evening comes
    With Mum's hair frizzing
Evening comes
    With TV blurring
Evening comes
    With Dad hurrying
Evening comes
    With the sun shining
Evening comes
    With Josh whining
Evening comes
    With me yawning
Evening comes
    With Mum nodding
Evening comes
    With midges itching
Evening comes
    With me fidgeting.

Kurtis Bann (9)
Fair Hill Primary School, Dromara

Afternoon

Afternoon comes
  With school bells ringing
Afternoon comes
  With birds singing
Afternoon comes
  With dogs barking
Afternoon comes
  With cows mooing
Afternoon comes
  With sun shining
Afternoon comes
  With TVs blurring
Afternoon comes
  With dinner cooking
Afternoon comes
  With homework solving
Afternoon comes
  With computers humming.

Peter Lathwell (8)
Fair Hill Primary School, Dromara

Mrs Clinghan

A teacher who is cool
The principal of school
Her arms swing
She wears a ring
Likes toffee
Drinks coffee
She never takes a chance
She takes traditional dance
Never lies
Orders all the supplies
Teaches classes
Wears glasses
She is always fair
And has short blonde hair
Always has something in mind
And she is very kind
She is really helpful
And *very* powerful!

Claire Hanna (9)
Fair Hill Primary School, Dromara

Summer

Summer comes
    With flowers blooming
Summer comes
    With children playing
Summer comes
    With farmers rolling
Summer comes
    With lambs growing
Summer comes
    With bees stinging
Summer comes
    With sun shining
Summer comes
    With people talking
Summer comes
    With water splashing.

Jackson Gill (9)
Fair Hill Primary School, Dromary

Summer Comes

Summer comes
   With sun shining
Summer comes
   With flowers blooming
Summer comes
   With children playing
Summer comes
   With joyful smiling
Summer comes
   With school closing
Summer comes
   With farmers bailing
Summer comes
   With holidays appearing
Summer comes
   With skin tanning.

Lauren Graham (9)
Fair Hill Primary School, Dromara

Animal Sounds And Movements

Elephants barge
Rhinos charge

Dogs bark
Monkeys lark

Lions roar
Larks soar

Camels hump
Kangaroos jump

Cows moo
Sharks chew

Mice creep
Cats leap

Parrots squawk
But I walk!

Ryan Murphy (9)
Fair Hill Primary School, Dromara

Summer

Summer comes
  With children screaming loudly
Summer comes
  With people playing happily
Summer comes
  With flowers blooming beautifully
Summer comes
  With the sun shining brightly
Summer comes
  With holidays coming quickly
Summer comes
  With people swimming joyfully
Summer comes
  With beach balls bouncing wildly
Summer comes
  With bees buzzing noisily
Summer comes
  With flowers scenting lovely.

Joel Wilson (9)
Fair Hill Primary School, Dromara

Christmas

Christmas comes
    With children singing happily
Christmas comes
    With bells ringing loudly
Christmas comes
    With present-opening quietly
Christmas comes
    With dinner cooking slowly
Christmas comes
    With reindeer flying magically
Christmas comes
    With tinsel shining brightly
Christmas comes
    With snowmen-building carefully
Christmas comes
    With lights flickering silently
Christmas comes
    With cracker-pulling wildly.

Aaron Stewart (9)
Fair Hill Primary School, Dromara

Christmas

Christmas comes
    With snow falling
Christmas comes
    With pantomimes starting
Christmas comes
    With bells ringing
Christmas comes
    With tinsel shining
Christmas comes
    With presents opening
Christmas comes
    With dinner cooking
Christmas comes
    With turkey roasting
Christmas comes
    With kids munching
Christmas comes
    With people singing.

Luke Stuart (9)
Fair Hill Primary School, Dromara

Noises In School

We go into school at nine o'clock,
The ring of a bell,
The tick of a clock,
The ruffle of pages as a kid looks in a book,
With lots of animations,
Just take a look.

The laughing and screaming of kids in the playground,
Jumping and shouting they make lots of sounds,
All the boys and girls playing football,
The crying of children as they fall off a wall,
The screeching of the chalk when the teacher writes on
                                                  the blackboard,
Talking about Vikings with their long, shiny swords.

Then all the kids have their lunch,
Then they jump out in the playground all in a bunch,
The kids play with hula hoops, skipping ropes and slides,
Then they all jump in a line and go inside.

Then the kids write stories,
They scribble and scrabble and crumple and scrape,
Then they finish their stories,
They don't make a mistake!

Then the bell rings, jingles and roars,
Then all the kids jump out the doors,
The kids run across the roads and into their home,
Then there's a ring and Mum picks up the phone,
I go up to my bed at the end of the day,
Ready to go to school and hear lots of noises, the next day.

Aoife Thomas (9)
Gaelscoil Na Bhfál, Belfast

Underwater

Underwater wailing whales,
Splashing sharks looking for food,
You may not believe me, but you should,
That there is a fish which has a hood.

Sushi is a fish that you can slurp up raw,
Crisp, crunch, you remove the bones with a saw,
Fibre fabler a fish goes out of water,
Bursting bubbles from big animals,
Roaring submarines, with radio voices.

Scattering fish when their enemy comes,
Trying to avoid those big, *giant* gulps,
Underneath ships there is a buzzing noise,
When you go diving underwater and you see a shipwreck,
You get memories of crunching, grinding, splashing and screaming,
When you come back up, *ziiipppp* goes your suit,
Then your boat skids off.

Aodhán Hughes (9)
Gaelscoil Na Bhfál, Belfast

Why?

Why don't you let us do art, teacher?
Why don't you let us be like Bart?
Why don't you let us run in class, teacher?
Why can't we play in a cart?

Why can't we lock you in a room, teacher?
Why can't we sing a rap?
Why can't I eat sweets, teacher?
Why can't I take a nap?

Why can't we fight, teacher?
Why can't I play with my toy gun?
Why can't we scream and shout, teacher?
Why can't we run into the sun?

Caolán Murphy (10)
Gaelscoil Na Bhfál, Belfast

Summer Is Here!

Summer is here,
Here comes the sun,
We can go to the beach
And have some fun.

Playing football every day,
Helps to pass the time away.
Playing with friends and having a good time,
Makes me glad the weather is fine.

Jordan O'Neill (11)
Gaelscoil Na Bhfál, Belfast

Anger

It is sore, red like a basketball bouncing on your head
It sounds like a car with no exhaust
It tastes like hot curry
It smells like burning rubber
It looks like Hell
It feels like getting shot
It reminds me of zombies.

Connall McStravick (10)
Gaelscoil Na Bhfál, Belfast

The Wind

The wind is chilly and cold all day,
I wouldn't want to go out to play
And the trees lose their leaves.
When Hallowe'en has come,
I run and have some fun.
When I see that school is here,
I run away and start to hum.

Caitlín Hunter (11)
Gaelscoil Na Bhfál, Belfast

The Wild

The wind swishing in the trees,
Lions roaring like mad,
The hippos drinking from the sea,
The monkeys are very sad.

The cheetah running in the grass,
The snakes are hissing, moving fast,
An ape tries to swing behind,
The dodo is the last.

Fintan Lowe (9)
Gaelscoil Na Bhfál, Belfast

Football

Football is my favourite game
Other teams are so lame
Liverpool is the best
Better than all the rest
As the keeper kicks the ball
A large cheer goes out by all
A goal is scored
The crowd roared
We won!

Aidan Manning (11)
Gaelscoil Na Bhfál, Belfast

Spring

S pring is here
P lease all cheer
R unning about in the sun
I will have lots of fun
N o teachers around
G o make a big sound.

Frankie Manning (10)
Gaelscoil Na Bhfál, Belfast

Life

Life,
No one can really explain,
What it is for.
Is it just to be a person
Or is it much more?

Is it so you can have fun
Or to see how well you can do?
I do both
My whole life through.

But why is it there,
Does anyone know?
Is it just to be there,
To walk to and fro?

Could it be to work hard,
Or to party all night?
There is no point in thinking,
Because no one knows what life is about!

Niamh Brennan (11)
Gaelscoil Na Bhfál, Belfast

Happiness

It is yellow, like a shiny diamond pointing at the sun,
Sounds like happy children playing in the park all day,
Tastes like melting chocolate in your mouth,
Smells like a lovely rose growing in the sun,
Looks like a summer day,
Feels like bubble wrap
Reminds me of a song called 'The Rose'.

Deirbhile Liggett (10)
Gaelscoil Na Bhfál, Belfast

Back To School

Back to school
All the teachers rule
It's great
Except when you're late
I am good
But not in the mood
I'm happy
But the school dinners are sloppy
Work is bad
When I'm sad
Work is back
And I am feeling black!

Maria Tomaszko (10)
Gaelscoil Na Bhfál, Belfast

I'm The One

I'm the one that frightens you away.
I'm the one that doesn't come out to play.
I'm the one that's sometimes cheeky or shy.

I'm the one that cares a lot.
I'm the one who shares a lot.
I'm the one that gets what I want.

I'm the one that has a best friend.
I'm the one that's full of trends.
I'm the one that loves … *me*.

Aoife Brannigan (10)
Gaelscoil Na Bhfál, Belfast

Going To The Funfair

Going to the funfair,
I'm jumping and thumping with joy,
People bump and thud in the line,
When you try to win a toy.

You see this very cool looking ride,
It goes high up in the air,
I get on it and it goes zooming fast,
And the wind rattles through your hair.

I feel a rumble in my tummy,
I get an ice cream cone,
I go over to my mum,
Then I realise it's time to go home.

I go to the car,
Then I slam the car door,
And I'm sad because,
I'm not in the funfair anymore.

Ciara O'Kane (9)
Gaelscoil Na Bhfál, Belfast

Celtic

Celtic, Celtic, champions again,
Celtic, Celtic, hail, hail.

A little bit of Iyaka with his speed,
A little bit of Miller is what we need.
A little bit of McManus in defence,
A little bit of McGeady, he's immense.
A little bit of Gordon, he's our man,
A little bit of singing from the fans.

Celtic, Celtic, champions again,
Celtic, Celtic, hail, hail.

Ciaran Keenan (11)
Gaelscoil Na Bhfál, Belfast

Noises At School

We walk into the school,
We hear the bell,
Children think it is very cool.

We hear some chalk falling on the floor,
Children shouting,
As we close the door.

Now people are writing stories,
I can't do mine because I can hear big, noisy lorries,
Clitter,
Clatter,
Chitter,
Chatter,
The bang of the door,
The thump of the chairs,
Now we are talking about big brown bears.

Aislinn Toal (9)
Gaelscoil Na Bhfál, Belfast

Week Of Winter Weather

On Monday there was *rain,*
It was such a pain.

On Tuesday there was *fog* and *frost,*
When I stepped out, I got lost.

On Wednesday *snow* was falling,
And all the cars were stalling.

On Thursday it was *freezing,*
It was so cold, I started sneezing.

On Friday *hailstones* fell down,
And hit the ground without a sound.

Ryan Toal (11)
Gaelscoil Na Bhfál, Belfast

Ann, The Teacher

Ann is sweet
Extraordinarily kind
If we do something bad
She doesn't mind.

Ann is sweet
As sweet as a sound
She is tall and thin
Instead of small and round.

Ann is sweet
With a century-old car
It is so old
It doesn't drive far.

Ann is sweet
She is here in the day
She is so nice to us
We wish she could stay.

Lauren Kerr (10)
Gaelscoil Na Bhfál, Belfast

Spooky Lady

A woman in green,
Looks nothing but mean,
Wearing green a lot.

She gets left out
And that's why she's hurt,
Being left on her own all day.

She tastes her sick,
She's as thin as a stick,
She's getting closer to death.

She's nothing but nasty,
She speaks very fastly,
They call her the Green Lady.

Vanessa Millen (10)
Gaelscoil Na Bhfál, Belfast

Colours In My Head!

Red is the smell of roses,
Red is the taste of raspberries,
Red is the feeling of anger.

Blue is the smell of mints,
Blue is the taste of chewing gum,
Blue is the feeling of coldness.

Purple is the smell of lavender,
Purple is the taste of plums,
Purple is the feeling of embarrassment.

Pink is the smell of pink roses,
Pink is the taste of candyfloss,
Pink is the feeling of excitement.

Yellow is the smell of daisies,
Yellow is the taste of bananas,
Yellow is the feeling of hotness.

Brown is the smell of hot melted chocolate,
Brown is the taste of chocolate,
Brown is the feeling of sickness.

Green is the smell of limes,
Green is the taste of green grapes,
Green is the feeling of happiness.

Grey is the smell of a dirty elephant,
Grey is the taste off muck,
Grey is the feeling of sickness.

Black is the smell of smoke,
Black is the taste of burned toast,
Black is the feeling of tiredness.

These are the colours in my head!

Seánagh Booth (10)
Gaelscoil Na Bhfál, Belfast

Summer Senses

Summer feels like petals on flowers
Very soft and sweet, oh the flowers
Summer tastes like strawberries
Sweet yet sour, very nice indeed
Summer sounds like birds singing
A very peaceful and beautiful sound
Summer looks like graceful trees
Lots and lots and lots of leaves
Summer smells like a delicate rose
The most beautiful smell I know.

Paula Tomaszko (11)
Gaelscoil Na Bhfál, Belfast

Spring

S pring is sunny and bright,
P eople warm in morning and night,
R eading quietly in the park,
 I n evening shadows growing dark,
N ow I look from my window,
G reen trees and flowers grow.

Shannon Duffy (10)
Gaelscoil Na Bhfál, Belfast

Morning

Morning comes with it singing and full of sun.
Morning comes with the lambs skipping and leaping.
Morning comes with the cows mooing.
Morning comes with a milkman whistling.
Morning comes with Dad feeding the cows.
Morning comes with the kettle singing.

Thomas McIlwaine (7)
Gortin Primary School, Gortin

My dog

My dog
    Loves to go walking
My dog
    Is amazing
My dog
    At the moon she is looking
My dog
    With cats she goes chasing
My dog
    With me likes to go running
My dog
    Likes to run around buildings.

Jacob McIlwaine (8)
Gortin Primary School, Gortin

Night-Time

Night-time comes
    With darkness falling
Night-time comes
    With stars shining brightly
Night-time comes
    With the moon shining.

Scott McNally (7)
Gortin Primary School, Gortin

Night-Time

Night-time comes
    With darkness falling
Night-time comes
    With bright stars shining
Night-time comes
    With silver moon shining.

Luci McKeown (7)
Gortin Primary School, Gortin

My Granny Woods

My granny is like a superhero to me,
I love to visit her when I can.
Granny loves me and I love her,
Granny listens to me when I speak to her.
I love my granny a lot.

She is beautiful and kind,
My granny is the best.
I want to visit as often as I can,
I love my granny a lot.

She buys me beautiful presents,
I love them a lot.
I read them and play with them,
They are so beautiful.
I love my granny a lot.

I can take them away anywhere I want to,
If I am allowed to take them with me.
Oh, I love my granny so much, oh so very much,
I love her with all my heart.
I love my granny a lot.

Aimee Porter (9)
Gortin Primary School, Gortin

The Rain

The rain is like tiny tears
Falling out of Heaven
With every little drop that falls
There is a reason why
With tears of joy and tears of sadness
There will be tears
As long as there is madness.

Jade Brown (8)
Gortin Primary School, Gortin

Night

Night comes
    Owls hooting in the night
Night comes
    When lights light up in the night
Night comes
    When children go to bed
Night comes
    When birds go to sleep
Night comes
    When shops close at 10pm
Night comes
    When rabbits go to sleep
Night comes
    When milkmen go to sleep.

David Adair (9)
Gortin Primary School, Gortin

Pride

Pride is like a bee
When it's made a pot of honey

Pride is like a joke you've said
And people think it's funny

Pride is when you've won a race
Miles before the others

Pride is like a cake you've made
And it's better than your mother's.

Anna Lonergan (11)
Holy Family Primary School, Teconnaught

Happiness

Happiness looks like a lollipop,
All round and sticky at the top.
Happiness sounds like your favourite track,
The disc at the top of the CD rack!
Happiness feels all warm and ready,
Like your new, big brown teddy.
Happiness tastes like a sweet in a shop,
Strawberry bubblegum that goes pop!
Happiness smells like newly baked bread,
Let's feast, who cares what Mum said!
Happiness reminds me of Dairy Milk chocolate,
Secretly stuffed into my pocket.

Annie Duffy (11)
Holy Family Primary School, Teconnaught

Anger

Anger feels like something tearing you apart inside.
Anger sounds like a cruel voice forcing you to do something.
Anger looks like a wee devil on fire.
Anger tastes like losing a Cup Final.
Anger smells like a burning fire.
Anger reminds me of doing sprints and jumps.

Aaron McClements (11)
Holy Family Primary School, Teconnaught

Excitement

Excitement sounds like your favourite music playing.
Excitement looks like fireworks exploding in the night sky.
Excitement tastes like my mum's cooking, straight out of the oven.
Excitement smells like cantering across the beach in the fresh

salt air.

Excitement feels like butterflies in my stomach.

Sinead Boyd (11)
Holy Family Primary School, Teconnaught

Excitement

Excitement looks like fireworks exploding into the night sky.
Excitement feels like something exploding deep inside.
Excitement sounds like a volcano erupting in thin air.
Excitement tastes like triple chocolate ice cream melting on
my tongue.
Excitement smells like daffodils on a fresh spring morning, when
a light breeze blows.
Excitement reminds me of my first ever Hallowe'en.

Niamh Darling (11)
Holy Family Primary School, Teconnaught

Happiness

Happiness looks like a multicoloured lollipop.
Happiness feels like a shiver up and down your spine.
Happiness sounds like a merry-go-round.
Happiness tastes like bubblegum and sugar plum.
Happiness smells like the first spring morning.
Happiness reminds me of going to Turkey on my holidays.

Síonon Selfe (11)
Holy Family Primary School, Teconnaught

Anger

Anger feels like blowing up inside of you.
Anger looks like a kettle has boiled up inside of you.
Anger tastes like a really bad type of food you eat.
Anger reminds me of when somebody says bad things to you.
Anger smells like a horrible type of water.
Anger sounds like a firework going off.

Conor Brannigan (11)
Holy Family Primary School, Teconnaught

Joy

Joy sounds like people cheering.
Joy looks like people playing.
Joy feels like Christmas morning.
Joy smells like a big steak for me.
Joy reminds me of my birthday.
Joy tastes like a big ice cream.

Connor Casement (11)
Holy Family Primary School, Teconnaught

Snake - Haiku

Snake hiding below
It is now ready to strike
On its rodent prey.

Niall Doherty (11)
Holy Family Primary School, Teconnaught

In The Flowerpot - Haiku

In the flowerpot
Blowing by the winter air
Blooming everywhere.

Victoria Byrne (11)
Holy Family Primary School, Teconnaught

Stars - Haiku

Shooting, dancing stars
High up above in the sky
In the dead of night.

Helen Smyth (11)
Holy Family Primary School, Teconnaught

Loneliness

Loneliness tastes like a sour, bitter sweet
Loneliness sounds like a big loud shriek
Loneliness looks like an ugly old witch
Loneliness feels like you are stuck in a ditch
Loneliness smells like an out of date Revel
Loneliness reminds me of the Devil.

Christopher Rice (11)
Holy Family Primary School, Teconnaught

People - Haiku

Different people
Some are Irish or English
They are who they are!

Caitriona Carville (11)
Holy Family Primary School, Teconnaught

On One Christmas Night - Haiku

On one Christmas night
My cat had a kitten! Aww!
It was really cute.

Niamh McCullough (11)
Holy Family Primary School, Teconnaught

Run Dog, Run - Haiku

In a clean garden
The dog is messing it up
Owner . . . run dog, run!

Alisha Hogg (11)
Holy Family Primary School, Teconnaught

Happiness

Happiness tastes like a big chocolate chip ice cream
Happiness smells like a water park
Happiness looks like a fun park
Happiness feels like a big laugh
Happiness reminds me of a holiday
Happiness sounds like fun.

Shane Rodgers (10)
Holy Family Primary School, Teconnaught

Happiness

Happiness looks like burning fire
Happiness feels like lovely hearts
Happiness sounds like singing birds
Happiness tastes like a lovely chocolate
Happiness smells like a red rose.

Ben Casement (10)
Holy Family Primary School, Teconnaught

Haiku

Clouds in the bright sky
Floating, next day flying by
Clouds fading away.

Aidan McDonald (11)
Holy Family Primary School, Teconnaught

Fun - Haiku

Children having fun
Having fun while in the sun
Messing around - fun!

Sarah Green (10)
Holy Family Primary School, Teconnaught

Young Writers - Little Laureates Inspirations From Northern Ireland

Frustration!

Frustration sounds like cars beeping their horns.
Frustration tastes like tasteless food.
Frustration smells like burning smoke.
Frustration looks like your team getting beaten.
Frustration feels like you can't do anything.
Frustration reminds me of Liverpool losing the Champions League.

Eoin Curran (11)
Holy Family Primary School, Teconnaught

Loneliness

Loneliness looks like bombs coming down on your house.
Loneliness feels like bullies hitting you with bats.
Loneliness sounds like nothing because there's nobody there.
Loneliness tastes like a very sour sweet.
Loneliness smells like boredom because there's nothing to do.
Loneliness reminds me of being left out, they're all running away.

Daniel McGreevy (11)
Holy Family Primary School, Teconnaught

Anger

Anger looks like red-hot, bubbling lava
Anger feels like a big needle being stabbed into me
Anger sounds like a nuclear bomb
Anger tastes like a red-hot chilli pepper
Anger smells like thick black smoke
Anger reminds me of the Devil.

John Patrick Convery (11)
Holy Family Primary School, Teconnaught

Laughter

Laughter is bright red and brown,
Like a little child's joyful smile,
When eating chocolate at the park,
On a warm summer's day.

It smells like fresh maple syrup
From the mountains of Canada,
On your tasty, scrumptious toasted pancakes,
Making you smile with every mouthful.

It tastes like the sweet victory of a football team
Winning the Champions League
For the first time in their history,
What a happy occasion!

It reminds me of a jolly clown,
Getting hit on the head with a custard pie,
At the crazy circus,
How the children laugh.

Laughter sounds like a baby giggling,
Shaking its rattle,
While watching its favourite cartoon
And throwing its toys
When bad guys come.

Laughter looks like a cheeky monkey,
Riding a unicycle around your bedroom,
While beeping a horn
With its eyes closed.

There's nothing else I can say,
You might die of laughter,
And I hope you laugh today.

Joshua Campbell & Tyler Young (10)
Millington Primary School, Portadown

It's Revenge

Revenge is red, like bloodshed
When your victim hits the ground
Your heart starts to pound

It reminds me of that fire burning inside
You wanna hit back
But you know you can't
Because you're gonna get in trouble
What are you gonna do?

It looks like a roaring fire concealed in the dark
But it will come out
There's no doubt about that

It tastes like sugar
Lovely and sweet
Makes your heart beat
The adrenalin rush, you can't get enough

It feels like your heart's pumping power
You think you're invincible
But you're not!

It sounds like a gun
Two sounds - *bang, bang!*
Now you're dead
Fifty bullets in your head

It smells like fire
What more can I say
It's revenge . . . how sweet.

Aaron Agnew (10)
Millington Primary School, Portadown

Silence

Silence is grey like
A small, dark room
Dull and bleak
Sitting all alone.

It smells like
The cold wind
On a moor
Only the wind.

Silence reminds me
Of some sad times
With no one to help
Only me.

It feels like
A pillow
None to disturb
None to wake . . .

Silence looks like
A small, sad face
Standing alone
Nothing but silence.

It sounds like
A mourning wail
From a loved one
In the distance.

Silence tastes like
Icy water
No one to love
Nothing there at all.

Megan Henry (10)
Millington Primary School, Portadown

Silence

Silence is white like
Snow
As it
Falls.

It smells like
Flowers
In a grassy
Meadow.

Silence reminds me
Of a phone call
With nobody on
The other end.

It feels like
A Persian cat's
Soft fur as
I stroke it.

Silence looks like
A kitten
Separated
From family.

It sounds like nothing
At all . . .
Just silence!

Joy Taylor (10)
Millington Primary School, Portadown

Happiness

Happiness is like . . .
Warm air
It smells like hot chocolate
It looks like a bright blue sky
It sounds like a lovely breeze
It reminds me of friendship
It tastes like candyfloss
It feels soft, cold and lovely
It falls from the sky like a falling star
It flies in the breeze like a paper aeroplane
It goes through your heart
And makes you realise that happiness is forever.

Jemma McCullough (10)
Millington Primary School, Portadown

Grandad

When I was new in the nursery,
The photographer took a photo of me.

My grandad found it
And said he'd keep it
And he still has that photo of me.

Today my hair is longer,
My grown-up teeth are here,
I now have scars all over my arms,
From exploring my backyard.

I don't have that silly old smile,
I don't have that stupid old cry.
But I'm still Grandad's little sweety pie.

Laura Donnelly
Our Lady's & St Mochua's Primary School, Derrynoose

My Chocolate Puppy

My chocolate puppy
Is a chocolate Lab
He plays with me
In the garden.

He is starting to teethe
And starting to chew
Just like a normal pup would do
We give him lots of squeaky toys
We give him balls to chew
But the one thing he always sneaks out with
Is Daddy's good leather shoes!

Fáinché Murphy (9)
Our Lady's & St Mochua's Primary School, Derrynoose

My New Sister

Her name is Codi Jo,
She has little tiny toes.
She has lots of hair on her head,
I give her my little bear
And she sits in her cuddly chair
And I always take care of her.

Síoneen McMahon (8)
Our Lady's & St Mochua's Primary School, Derrynoose

My Mother

She looks like a red rose.
She feels so gentle.
She sounds like a harp.
She smells like a bottle of perfume.
She touches like a delicate rose petal.
She reminds me of a rose.

Eryn Murphy (9)
Our Lady's & St Mochua's Primary School, Derrynoose

My Troublemaker

I have a troublemaker,
Alright, he's in my books,
He's in my dinner,
In my face,
In my school bag,
All the time.

I love my troublemaker,
When he's in bed,
Snoring, wrapped up in bed,
Oh how I wish it was
Like this all the time.

He always seems to
Get his own way,
Oh, I wish it was me.

But I'm not one.

Gabrielle Fox (9)
Our Lady's & St Mochua's Primary School, Derrynoose

Owls

The owl sits upon a tree
Way up high where nobody can see
He lives his life in harmony.

He hunts all night
Looking for worms, beetles, mice, insects
He looks quite fat, feathery
He makes a tu-whit tu-whoo sound
He can turn his head around.

Kelly McMahon (9)
Our Lady's & St Mochua's Primary School, Derrynoose

My Little Cousin

My little cousin
He screams and screams all day
He always gets his way
Every single day.

My little cousin
Do you want to play?
My little cousin
Today will be OK.

My little cousin
Stop stealing my fun
My little cousin
Look at the shiny sun.

My little cousin
Go and play with cars
While I go . . .
And escape to Mars.

Carolyn Fitzpatrick (9)
Our Lady's & St Mochua's Primary School, Derrynoose

Padraig

P adraig is a good boy
A lways plays football
D ogs are his favourite pet
R eally enjoys eating chicken
A t home he watches TV
I nterested in horses
G ood boy!

Padraig Renaghan (8)
Our Lady's & St Mochua's Primary School, Derrynoose

Spring Poem

Spring is green grass and shiny sun.
It tastes like warm air and Easter eggs.
It sounds like children playing in the grass
And tractors mowing the fields.
It looks like bluebells in the fields and newborn animals.
It smells like lovely flowers and fresh air.
It makes me feel jolly good and free.

Ciara Mallon (9)
Our Lady's & St Mochua's Primary School, Derrynoose

Spring Poem

Spring is shiny yellow and dazzling blue.
It tastes like yummy Easter eggs and breezy air.
It sounds like pretty birds tweeting and little children playing.
It looks like everyone is really happy and baby animals feel great.
It smells really fresh and joyful.
It makes me feel happy and free.

Rebecca McNaughton (7)
Our Lady's & St Mochua's Primary School, Derrynoose

Spring Poem

Springtime is wonderful and great.
It tastes like sunshine and air.
It sounds like breeze and children playing.
It looks like new animals and a good time.
It smells like joy and freshness.
It makes me feel really good and funny.

James Murray (9)
Our Lady's & St Mochua's Primary School, Derrynoose

My Dog Patch

I want to give him hugs and kisses

L oving dog is mine
O ver the moon is my dog when he sees food
V ery good, that is my dog
E veryone loves my dog, he is just the best

P ops out of nowhere
A t dinner time he jumps and jumps
T here is a time when he can be silly
C ute are his little eyes
H e is the best dog ever and he's mine

Marie-Claire Burke (9)
Our Lady's & St Mochua's Primary School, Derrynoose

Ferrari

F erraris are so fast
E ating through the other cars
R oaring so loud
R evving for its win
A cting like a man's favourite thing
R oaring and cheering for it
I n the fastest car's place.

Shane Donnelly (9)
Our Lady's & St Mochua's Primary School, Derrynoose

Lucky

L is for my lovely dog who licks me to show his love
U is for upset - he rests his head on his paws
C is for cute, his big brown eyes looking at me
K is for kind, letting me play hoop without biting it
Y is for yellow, the colour of my dog, Lucky, a beautiful
                                            Border collie.

Shannon McGuigan (9)
Our Lady's & St Mochua's Primary School, Derrynoose

Teachers

Teachers give me homework
Teachers give me work
Teachers give me playtime
That will work!

Teachers give me dinner
Teachers give me lunch
Sometimes they even give me
A little bit of brunch.

Teachers give me information
Teachers give me space
Teachers give me fun activities
And all the games.

Teachers give me plaques
Teachers give me merit marks
We only get them if we're good
Teachers tell me to improve myself.

Ellen Hamilton (8)
Our Lady's & St Mochua's Primary School, Derrynoose

My Toothbrush

My toothbrush is no good
My toothbrush is cool
My toothbrush nice and clean
My toothbrush green fighting medicine
My toothbrush helps me with my gums
Fighting smelly breath

My toothbrush is bendy
My toothbrush is seen
My toothbrush does not like toothpaste
But it is clean.

Gareth Whyte (9)
Our Lady's & St Mochua's Primary School, Derrynoose

Homework, Homework

Homework, homework,
Not much fun
Apple sauce and bubblegum.
Trying hard to learn to spell,
Makes my brain begin to swell.

Homework, homework,
Really smells.
Chocolate cake and caramel,
Never want to be a cheat,
In case I never get a treat.

So homework, homework
Why can't you be
Just like sweets
Or just like me?

Alice Lennon (8)
Our Lady's & St Mochua's Primary School, Derrynoose

My Hot-Water Bottle

My hot-water bottle is black as a rat
It's hot, hot, hot just like my cat.

My bed is cold,
My feet are chilly,
I need some heat quickly!

It warms up my feet,
It warms up the bed,
It makes me feel hot up to my head.

Now I'm too hot -
I kick it out on the floor.

I wish I didn't have one
Because I would like my bed to be cold instead.

Bernice Conlon (9)
Our Lady's & St Mochua's Primary School, Derrynoose

Washing Machine

Weekend's here
Time to wash
Clothes all dirty
Washing machine ready
Powder's coming
Detergent too.

Turn it on
And away we go
Clicking, spinning
Round and round
Clothes are washing
Right about now.

Now the clothes
Are done and
Ready to be worn
Mummy's very happy
Because that's the
Washing gone!

Pauric McNaughton (9)
Our Lady's & St Mochua's Primary School, Derrynoose

Spring

Spring is light brown and nice yellow
It tastes like fresh sunshine and lovely eggs
It sounds like little birds and singing lambs
It smells like fresh grass
It makes me feel joyful and free.

Emma Mone (8)
Our Lady's & St Mochua's Primary School, Derrynoose

My Dog Dusty

My dog is happy
When she wags her tail.
When my dog is angry
She starts to rise her lip
And shows her sharp teeth.
When my dog is lonely
She lays down on the lane
And that's my dog Dusty.

Bronagh Downey
Our Lady's & St Mochua's Primary School, Derrynoose

My Dog

My dog is very jumpy,
Sometimes too much,
She seems to be very smelly.

She loves her dinner
And my mum,
But not so much me.

Keelin Boyd (9)
Our Lady's & St Mochua's Primary School, Derrynoose

Pearse

P earse is very fun
E ats up everything
A t school he's good
R abbits are his favourite pets
S weets are his favourite food
E mmet is his friend.

Pearse Lennon (8)
Our Lady's & St Mochua's Primary School, Derrynoose

My Dog

I have a dog
Whose name is Tog
He likes a match
Of friendly catch
He has a big house
As big as a mouse
He loves roses
Their flavour is lovely
He is very soft
He hides in our loft
Because of the mice
He tries to catch them
But really just gets lice.

Emma Rice (10)
Our Lady's & St Mochua's Primary School, Derrynoose

Animals

A creepy crocodile swims through the swamp,
When he goes to the shore he gets a bump,
And when the fish come out to play,
They'll all be scared away.

A troublesome tiger jumps into a tree,
While he was looking for his tea,
Along comes a deer,
And he waits for it to come near.

A graceful giraffe looks over the treetop,
And while he did so,
A kangaroo went hop, hop, hop down below.

Catherine Anne Nugent (8)
Our Lady's & St Mochua's Primary School, Derrynoose

My Granny

My granny is over 21
I go over to see her every day
We have lots of fun
And love to play
She loves to bake buns and tarts
She lives across from Carnagh forest.

She loves to garden every day
Then at night she kneels to pray
When I go over to stay at night
She boils the kettle and we eat some delights.

Granny makes me smile and laugh
As I watch her skip up the path
Thank God for my granny.
The best granny in the world.

Dína Heavin (9)
Our Lady's & St Mochua's Primary School, Derrynoose

Summer Holidays

School term coming to an end,
Summer holidays just round the bend.
Sunshine, smiles and lots of fun,
Lots of time for lots of sun.

The ice cream's melting,
Good job the rain's not pelting.
Summer fun at the BBQ,
Another burger? Merci beaucoup!

Eimear McCarthy (8)
Our Lady's & St Mochua's Primary School, Derrynoose

Summer

It's nearly the summer
And school's nearly over.
I will be able to play
With a horse called Clover.
I can't wait till the day
That I will hear the last bell ring.
The bell might be fast
But it will ring with a blast.
A joyful time to hear it ring
I might even want to sing.
How boring school is
I just want to start snoring till summer.

Sinead McKee (10)
Our Lady's & St Mochua's Primary School, Derrynoose

Summer

School is almost over
I can't wait till then
When I hear the last bell ring
I'll be free from history
The summer days have come
I feel a lot of fun
Sometimes I just want to run, run, run!
I never stop, even to eat a bun
As the sun sets and goes down
My fun goes up, up, up!
Into the dark night sky.

Orla Breen (10)
Our Lady's & St Mochua's Primary School, Derrynoose

Summer

I can't wait till the summer,
The winter is so much duller,
When I am sick,
The time doesn't go so quick.

During the summer days,
I go on a holiday,
When I come out of the plain,
I get up and scream.

Back on the plane,
I go home with Shane,
So bright and colourful,
As the end of the day dulls,
I unpack my case,
So neat and tidy,
As I go off to sleep,
For the new day coming.

Martina McNally (10)
Our Lady's & St Mochua's Primary School, Derrynoose

Summer

Summer is the best
But there is less
Fun in summer
So it's a bit of a bummer
When school is back
To routine again
So again rain pours
Down heavily
I hope school is
Better than summer
But if it isn't
They are both a bummer.

Jennifer Lynch (9)
Our Lady's & St Mochua's Primary School, Derrynoose

Summer

Summer is coming!
Yes, yes!
Glorious summer mornings to enjoy,
Going on school trips!
Playing outside!
These are the things that I
Rejoice in!

Going to the shop!
Bike rides!
Going to the pool,
Summer in Salou.
These are the things I love
About summer!

Michael McGrane (10)
Our Lady's & St Mochua's Primary School, Derrynoose

Summer

Summer is the best,
It's better than all the rest,
Better than school,
It's very, very cool.

When I'm outside,
I'd never wish to be inside,
On those horrible days of school,
I'd rather go to the pool,
In Salou.

Summer is just great,
But I still miss my mates.

Hannah Finnegan (10)
Our Lady's & St Mochua's Primary School, Derrynoose

Hallowe'en

Hallowe'n is my favourite time of year
Ghosts and ghouls fill us with fear
In the night
The bangs give me a fright!

The fireworks make a big bang
The witches flying through the skies
I hope I do not get caught by one of them
I am all tucked up in bed
I do not have to worry.

Christine Hart (10)
St Brendan's Primary School, Craigavon

Tubby

Tubby is my cuddly, buddly beast
He comes to me in my dreams
And we have a big feast.
Tall and round, his face is shaped like a pound
And I love him when he makes his musical sound.
Tubby can only be seen by me,
That's why he's special and cute,
All for little me.

Orla Lamph (10)
St Brendan's Primary School, Craigavon

Sharana

S harana is the king of the land
H e can eat two people at once
A shark and piranha head with
R azor-sharp teeth
A multicoloured body
N othing can destroy him
A true killer is . . .
    Sharana.

Christopher Fitzsimmons (10)
St Brendan's Primary School, Craigavon

The Hallowe'n Fright

Fireworks and sparkles light up the sky
Bonfires roar as the flames fly up high.
Everyone shouting, 'Trick or treat?'
With loads to eat on Hallowe'en night.
Zombies, ghouls and ghosts too,
Like to scare and shout out *boo!*
But beware, you never can tell,
What they'll do to you.
    Happy Hallowe'en

Rhiannon Haughian (10)
St Brendan's Primary School, Craigavon

Witches Flying In The Sky

Witches flying in the sky,
Be careful you don't catch their eye.
They can see you from miles away
And can kill you in less than one day.

So take my advice
And always think twice,
Don't think that they can't see you,
You just don't know what they can really do!

Alana Hughes (10)
St Brendan's Primary School, Craigavon

Life And Death

Red of blood, pouring out from the wound.
Yellow of the light, shining gates of Heaven.
Orange of the flowers, laid upon the grave.
Blue of the shining sky, where your soul lives forever.
Green of the grass, of the grass beside your gravestone.
Indigo of the tears, from others' eyes.
Violet of the flowers, planted beside you.

Luke Devlin (9)
St Brendan's Primary School, Craigavon

The Boy Who Told No Lies

There was a little boy who couldn't tell a lie,
Even though it meant he couldn't look people in the eye.

He told his granny he didn't like her dress,
He told his mum her house was a mess.

He told his teacher the lesson was boring,
He told his granda he wouldn't stop snoring.

Then one day he told the truth and made his best friend cry,
Then he realised sometimes it was better to tell a lie.

Ellie McKeagney (9)
St Brendan's Primary School, Craigavon

Dirty Pig

In the sty the pig lies, for a nice little nap,
He loves to wallow about in the dirty mud,
It's like a bath to him.
He dives down deep into the mud,
He rolls like a demon in the dirty brown mud.
He climbs out of the mud pool
And sleeps in the sun to let the muck dry.
When he wakes up, he stretches his legs and yawns,
He eats like a monster and gobbles everything in his barrel up.

Caolan Gormley (10)
St Joseph's Primary School, Caledon

What Is Snow Like?

Snow is a white sheet
Snow is lots of tiny white footballs kicked around
Snow is buckets of papers spread round the world
Snow is millions of cotton balls
Snow is rubbers falling from the sky
Snow is handfuls of white boards falling everywhere.

Louise Carey (9)
St Joseph's Primary School, Caledon

Rabbits

Rabbits like to sit in the sun,
With their babies out having fun,
The mum rabbit feeds her kit,
Then lets her kit out to sit.
She calls her in for some food,
She eats it up, it's really good,
Then they both fall asleep
And don't seem to let out a peep.

Erin McCausland (9)
St Joseph's Primary School, Caledon

The Owl

I see an owl in the tree,
He prepares to fly, 1, 2, 3.
He spots a rat,
He's going to dive,
He swoops it up and then he glides.
His baby is hungry, he wants some food,
They share the rat and then they snooze.

Ciaran Shevlin (9)
St Joseph's Primary School, Caledon

What Is The Moon?

The moon is a ball of white bouncing around the world.
The moon is a giant lighthouse whirling.
The moon is a massive plate ready to be eaten from.
The moon is God's football leaping in space.
The moon is a fat clock showing its time.
The moon is a colossal shooting star turning all about.

Clare McKenna (11)
St Joseph's Primary School, Caledon

Monkeys

Deep in the forest,
The monkeys in the trees,
Eating birds' eggs,
Yes, they might have fleas.

Monkeys are good climbers
And they live in troops,
They call their mates,
In different groups.

They eat small insects
And plants too,
It's such a pity
To see them in a zoo.

The cheeky monkeys,
Climb, swing and hop,
While others sit,
Right up at the top.

Kerry Hornsey (10)
St Joseph's Primary School, Caledon

Fishy

Fishy, fishy in the sea
Come and swim over to me.

Don't bite my toes
Don't lick my knees
Just swim beside me.

The sun is hot, the water is warm
The fishy and me play all day long.

Kelli Loughran (11)
St Joseph's Primary School, Caledon

Cinderella

Dusty clothes and filthy hair,
Her feet are swollen, cold and bare.
For it's Cinderella all alone,
Cleaning the dusty telephone.

Her ugly stepsisters enter in,
And start emptying the rubbish bin.
Poor Cinderella, more dust to clean,
Her stepsisters are so ugly and mean.

Catherine O'Gorman (10)
St Joseph's Primary School, Caledon

Hamster

She stares at me with her eyes like beads
She eats her nuts and her sunflower seeds
She runs on her wheel at night
But falls asleep in daylight
She wakes up when the moon comes out
She climbs in her ball and runs about.

Kevin Magnone (11)
St Joseph's Primary School, Caledon

Fishy

Swimming around like a mad monkey,
Searching for a way to escape,
Like a trapped prisoner in a cell,
Looking for a secret door,
Like a sneaky fox trying to catch a rabbit.
Goldfish trapped in a bowl,
Wishing it were free.

Caoimhe Hughes (11)
St Joseph's Primary School, Caledon

Animals

Pandas jump, caterpillars hump
Lions stalk, birds talk
Seagulls glide, owls hide
Cats creep, lions leap
Rabbits bounce, kittens pounce
Frogs hop, horses clop
Elephants run and I have fun.

Luke Sherry (9)
St Joseph's Primary School, Caledon

Animals

Snails slide, pandas hide,
Birds flap, horses lap,
Lions stalk, turtles walk,
Birds sing, frogs fling,
Pigs grunt, lions hunt,
Monkeys climb, snails leave slime,
Leopards run, kittens have fun,
Monkeys chatter, hippos get fatter,
Crabs snap, monkeys clap,
Chickens cluck, sheep buck.

Patrick McKenna (9)
St Joseph's Primary School, Caledon

Captive Hamster

Racing on its wheel all night,
Nibbling and nibbling away till daylight.
His little mind dreams about a different day,
That lucky day he'll creep away.

Siobhan Wray (11)
St Joseph's Primary School, Caledon

The Little Liar

Rachel Cary was a dreadful liar,
Every day her lies got higher.
When she is told to do her chores,
She pretends to sleep and loudly snores!

She rings the fire brigade on 999,
When her parents aren't home, she hides all their wine.
When her mother asks her, 'Who did this?'
She makes up lies like, 'It was the big sis.'

Her mother grows bad-tempered, when Rachel tells a lie,
But she just puts on a sad face and pretends to cry.
Her father comes in and exclaims, 'Why do you always lie?'
And her reply is, 'I don't know why.'

Her mother walks off and Father is left to speak,
He said, 'You know, if you lie any more you'll grow a beak!'
Rachel laughed so hard she made the house shake,
But by next morning she had a beak the size of a lake!

Sarah-Louise Hughes (10)
St Joseph's Primary School, Caledon

Rooney

Rooney is the best footballer in the land,
He plays with skill for his team, England,
He plays for Manchester United, the best team by far,
He can kick the ball with skill and power.

He has scored 11 international goals to date,
For more of these, we won't have long to wait,
He is the best footballer, watch him run,
Everyone knows he's simply number *one!*

Aaron Doherty (9)
St Mary's Primary School, Craigavon

If I Were An Artist

If I were an artist,
I'd paint the portrait
Of Jewel, the death-defying dragon!

For his body, a unicorn, colour of emerald,
For his head, a horse's with a blending of sapphire
And the splendour of the marigold.

He would have a shiny horn
In which you could see the magnificence of the ocean,
Blue and deep.

For his eyes, the colour and innocence of the bluebell,
Shimmering with the jewel of the water
And the sweet scent of the lotus flower.

For his tail, gleaming silver strands sparkling like diamonds,
For his wings, fluffy clouds with jewels of all sorts
Shining through the mist.

And for his hands and feet, the hooves of a horse,
With the glitter sensation of the stars,
Shining down in a radiant light.

Miamph Hanlon (10)
St Mary's Primary School, Craigavon

My Cat

My cat sits quietly on the window sill
Nothing to do but lie so still.
She stares around for something nice
But all she spies are wee brown mice.
She throws them and tosses them about
She squeezes them till their eyes pop out!
She's a hungry cat, she likes to eat
These wee brown mice make a tasty treat!

Josh Kane (9)
St Mary's Primary School, Craigavon

The Storm

The wind it tapped my window,
It gave me a sore head,
I pulled my pillow over my head,
As I lay stiff and frightened in bed.

The thunder it started rumbling,
The lightning knocked down many trees,
Not a single bird was singing its song,
Nor were any of the bees.

I got up that night full of fear and dread,
Then I heard the deafening roar,
I just stood there still, not able to move,
As the storm crashed upon the shore.

The rain got heavier and heavier,
Huge big hailstones came tumbling down,
I jumped back under my duvet,
Still wearing my dressing gown!

The wind it tapped my window,
It gave me a sore head,
I pulled my pillow back over my head,
As I lay stiff and frightened in bed.

Caoimhe Bunting (10)
St Mary's Primary School, Craigavon

School Poem

My wee school is on the shores of Lough Neagh,
I enjoy going there every day.
Some of the pupils are very tall,
Some of them are still quite small,
But we all love doing PE in the hall.

We learn about science and history too,
We try our best in all that we do.
We have good fun with our friends each day,
In our wee school on the shores of Lough Neagh.

Cormac Lavery (9)
St Mary's Primary School, Craigavon

My Cat Tido

Tido was my cat,
But he wasn't very fat,
Sometimes he even looked like he was wearing a hat.

His fur was all scruffy,
It was black and white,
He used to sleep with me every night!

If there was a mouse, running round our house,
He would pounce and attack
And that mouse wouldn't come back!

Tido my cat loved to sit on a mat,
Sleeping by the fire as the flames rose higher.
I loved my wee cat with all my heart,
It makes me sad now that we're apart.

He's up in cat heaven now,
He died a year ago.
I will never forget him,
No matter where I go.

PJ McGarrity (10)
St Mary's Primary School, Craigavon

My House

Above my house is the big blue sky
This is where all the little birds fly.

Beside my house is my garden so green
Lovely flowers and trees can always be seen.

Below my house, deep underground
Are lots of mice who don't make a sound.

Inside my house my dad and brother
And of course there's me and my great mother!

Tiernan Kane-Cavanagh (9)
St Mary's Primary School, Craigavon

Ten Little Schoolgirls

(Based on 'Ten Little Schoolboys' by AA Milne)

Ten little schoolgirls standing in a line
One ran home and that left nine.

Nine smart schoolgirls standing by a gate
One jumped over it and that left eight.

Eight happy schoolgirls took a bus to Devon
One got run over and that left seven.

Seven fun schoolgirls eating a Twix
One was poisoned and that left six.

Six pretty schoolgirls learning to dive
One disappeared and that left five.

Five silly schoolgirls opened a door
One went in and that left four.

Four naughty schoolgirls climbed up a tree
One fell off and that left three.

Three tired schoolgirls went to the zoo
One got eaten and that left two.

Two shy schoolgirls lying in the sun
One got hot and that left one.

One little schoolgirl eating a bun
She ran off and that left none.

Rebecca Harbinson (9)
St Mary's Primary School, Craigavon

Ten Little Schoolboys

(Based on 'Ten Little Schoolboys' by AA Milne)

Ten little schoolboys standing in a line,
One ran home and then there were nine.

Nine smart schoolboys standing by the gate,
One jumped over it and that left eight.

Eight happy schoolboys took a bus to Devon,
One got run over and that left seven.

Seven cool schoolboys eating a Twix,
One got poisoned and that left six.

Six stupid schoolboys playing with a beehive,
One got stung and that left five.

Five sad schoolboys weeping on the floor,
One ran off and that left four.

Four tall schoolboys swimming in the sea,
One was eaten by a shark and that left three.

Three small schoolboys running round the zoo,
One got locked up and that left two.

Two cool schoolboys standing in the sun,
One got sunburn and that left one.

One lonely schoolboy, the last little hero,
He ran home to his mum and that left zero!

Caolan Farr (10)
St Mary's Primary School, Craigavon

Jump Or Jiggle?

Lions roar
Larks soar

Bees sting
Birds sing

Cats sleep
Frogs leap

Cows moo
Elephants poo

Owls stalk
Parrots talk

Eagles fly
Dogs cry

Goats fight
Leeches bite

Rabbits jump
Caterpillars hump

Seagulls glide
Penguins slide

Worms wriggle
But -
I just giggle!

Aaron Mooney (10)
St Mary's Primary School, Craigavon

Jump Or Jiggle?

Lions roar
Larks soar

Penguins slide
Eagles glide

Frogs hop
Horses clop

Cats pounce
Bunnies bounce

Bears defeat
Monkeys eat

Whales cry
Birds fly

Snakes slither
Dogs quiver

Donkeys bray
Puppies play

Caterpillars wiggle
Worms wriggle

Wolves walk
But -
I talk.

Molly Lavery (9)
St Mary's Primary School, Craigavon

Quality Street

Quality Street are wonderful,
Quality Street are great,
Quality Street are the sweetest sweets
God could ever create!

You should really taste 'em,
They really are a treat,
The best sweets in the whole wide world
Are called Quality Street.

I like the green triangles,
The Strawberry Dream is delicious too.
Who in the world wouldn't like them?
I could eat quite a few!

I like the Orange Crunch
And the Orange Cream,
They float down into my tummy,
Like a lovely chocolate stream.

I like the Strawberry Fudge,
Don't forget that Toffee Penny,
Whenever I see these sweets,
I always eat far too many!

So maybe when you come to visit
And want a bite to eat,
Would you ever be so kind
And bring a box of Quality Street?

Aoife McGuinness (9)
St Mary's Primary School, Craigavon

The Best Things At School

I love to write my stories,
And I don't mind numeracy,
Art is always brilliant,
So is geography!

In science we learn so many new things,
History is always fun too,
We love to write poems for literacy,
I just love school, don't you?

But best of all, my friends are all there,
They help me through each day,
We have so much fun together
In every possible way!

When it's all over and time to go home,
The bell rings out loud and clear,
I really don't mind going to school
Because I seem to get smarter each year!

Rebekah Clenaghan (9)
St Mary's Primary School, Craigavon

My Brother Wants A Pet

Every morning I hear whining, squealing for a pet.
My brother doesn't realise he's not going to get
A dog or a cat, a hamster or a mouse
He'll just have to be happy with me around the house.
I think it would be great to have a pet around the place
It might take the horrible scowl off his face!
The whining will go on for a year, maybe two
I don't think we'll ever get a pet, do you?

Monica McCavigan (9)
St Mary's Primary School, Craigavon

Schooldays!

Monday was quite alright,
We were just back from our break,
Our teacher was very pleased,
Because great progress we did make.

Tuesday was just normal,
Everyone was still really smart,
Because we had been so good all day,
We got to do some extra art.

Wednesday was the same,
Only I got all my sums *correct,*
Then we wrote some poems,
I hope mine is perfect!

Thursday was just Thursday,
We did some Alive-O,
No one got anything wrong,
So we didn't hear, 'No, no, no!'

Friday is my favourite day,
I think you'll all agree,
When the final bell rings at three on the dot,
Out the door I skip with glee!

Eimhear Bunting (10)
St Mary's Primary School, Craigavon

School

I like PE
I like doing art
My teacher says I'm very smart
I like doing sums
I like to sing
In fact I like doing everything
My school is right beside Lough Neagh
I love to go there every day.

Caoimhe Holden (9)
St Mary's Primary School, Craigavon

Above My House

Above my house
There's a big yellow sun
I watch it while I eat my bun
And then I play and have some fun.

Beside my house
There's a river flowing past
I love to paddle
And swim really fast.

Below my house
Is a deep dark hole
The only one living there
Is a wee, tiny mole.

Eunan Walsh (9)
St Mary's Primary School, Craigavon

Pigs

Pigs are smelly
Pigs are pink
Pigs are really cool I think.

Pigs eat porridge
With water in it
Mum doesn't like pigs
Not even a bit.

Pigs sleep in the mud
They play there too
I love pigs
Do you?

Kieran Lavery (10)
St Mary's Primary School, Craigavon

But Mum . . . But Dad . . .

'Mum, can I go to the shop please?'
'I don't know, ask your dad, Louise!'
'Dad, can I go to the shop? Mum said to ask you.'
'What are you looking for, you've got everything brand new?'
'So please, please can I go?'
'Ask your mum, she should know!'
Louise went back to her mum in the kitchen,
To find her mum sitting stitching.
'Mum, Mum, can I go? Dad said to ask you.'
'For God's sake! I don't know!'
'I only want to get a packet of sweets and a drink.'
'Oh alright, there's money in my purse I think.'
So off she went and on the way she met a boy and posed!
She was too busy in a world of her own.
By the time she got there, the shop was closed!

Holleah McNally (10)
St Mary's Primary School, Craigavon

My Teacher

My teacher teaches us all day
And if we are good, we get to play.
My teacher calls us by our own names
Sometimes she lets us play games.

My teacher is kind and usually happy
Sometimes she's cross and a wee bit snappy.
She rewards us when our work is good
This puts me in a really good mood.

My teacher has shiny black hair
She splits us into groups to be fair.
She teaches us so many things
When she's happy she always sings.

Leeanne Nelson (9)
St Mary's Primary School, Craigavon

Cats

I want a cat,
I want a cat,
A black and white and fluffy cat.
My mum said no,
So I started to cry,
If I don't get a cat, I will surely die!

Cats move slowly with such grace,
I want a cat with a wee cute face!
Cats like to stroll around the house,
Cats like to eat a juicy mouse!

I want a cat,
I want a cat,
A wee black and white fluffy cat!

Lisa Bunting (9)
St Mary's Primary School, Craigavon

My School

I have a little school, I go there every day,
It's on the shores of lovely Lough Neagh.

It's a fun place to go
It's a good place to play
I like to meet my friends there every single day!

There are lots of things to learn
And so much work to do,
Everyone tries their best
The whole day through!

It's a fun place to learn, St Mary's Derrymore
My wee school on the Lough Neagh shore!

Natasha Doone (9)
St Mary's Primary School, Craigavon

Animal Homes

Animal homes all sizes and shapes
Some of them square, some of them round.
Some animals live under the sea
Some of them live just under the ground.

Some animals live in burrows so deep
They crawl into safety at night to sleep.
Of course the fish live in the sea,
That's very different from you and me.

Then there's the fish who live in a bowl
Don't forget Badger in the deep, dark hole.
I'm glad my house is comfy and big
I'm glad I don't live in a sty with a pig!

Chloe Doone (9)
St Mary's Primary School, Craigavon

My Dog

My dog Fred,
Likes to eat bread,
He likes to go to bed,
But he doesn't like marmalade.

He plays with me,
When I am free,
Fred likes kiwi,
But not me.

Fred is fat,
He likes to sleep on a mat,
He likes treats
And he likes meat.

Conaire Lavery (10)
St Mary's Primary School, Craigavon

Chelsea

Jose, Jose, he's our man
If he can't do it, no one can
Lampard is the best
Man U don't have time to rest

Drogba will scare your keeper
Sir Alex will take a beamer
Terry's gonna lead us to victory
Robben said, 'You're blind, referee'

Cech is saving the team
With his incredible diving
A bit of Shauny with his speed
With Ballack we will achieve

Joe Cole is running down the wing
With his amazing tricks, he can do anything
A bit of Mikel in our lives
A bit of the fans on our side.

Sean Murphy (11)
St Patrick's Primary School, Downpatrick

Sports

I like football, it gets me excited,
I'd love to play for Celtic or Man United.

I don't like cricket, but I like to swim,
Any sport I play I like to win.

Gaelic and Hurley are hard to play,
I would like to play for Down someday.

By using my muscles and getting real fit,
I'll be a champion boxer with my two fists.

Daniel Kelly (11)
St Patrick's Primary School, Downpatrick

Fast Cars

Aston Martins, Ferraris and Maseratis,
Porsches, MGs and Bugattis.
Shiny paintwork, tyres of black,
Roaring engines, on a speedy track.

Lamborghinis are so cool
On the road they definitely rule.
They are supersonic
A real feel good tonic.

Maseratis are very fast
They can really whizz right past.
These cars can do 200 miles an hour
They give you super power.

Bugattis are the cream of the crop
For elegance they are always top.
They have a lot of speed and style
Their drivers enjoy every mile.

Manus Kelly (11)
St Patrick's Primary School, Downpatrick

Games Consoles

PS3 is Sony's console
It's black and silver and shiny
You can game, video and rock 'n' roll

Xbox 360 is a Microsoft machine
It's white with green and smooth
The owners say it's extreme

DS is a Nintendo compact
You can choose pink, black and blue
It is fun, fun, fun, that's a fact

Wii is Nintendo's superstar
It is white and blue and shiny too
I believe it's the best by far!

Conor Mullan (11)
St Patrick's Primary School, Downpatrick

Summer

The sun is shining brightly,
Everyone is running sprightly.
The bees are humming, humming,
Making lots of yummy honey.

The children are playing in the street,
In their bare feet.
The wind is gently blowing,
The river is constantly flowing.

The birds in the trees,
The humming of the bees.
The children's screams,
The parents' dreams.

On the swing,
There I sing,
Enjoying the day
And the last ray.

Mark Robinson (11)
St Patrick's Primary School, Downpatrick

United V Chelsea

Lampard goes to score his screamer,
Giggsy huffs and takes a beamer,
Van Der Sar lets it slip in,
Fergy shouts, 'We gotta win!'

Ronaldo passes it down the side,
Rooney gets it, the crowd goes wild,
Fletcher bangs it off his toe,
The ball goes in, the crowd shout, 'Goal!'

All in all it was a good game,
United won themselves the match,
Fergy jumped around with joy,
Mourinho sat and huffed like a boy.

Matthew Campbell (11)
St Patrick's Primary School, Downpatrick

Football

Football is my hobby
Football is the best
Football is so cool
It's better than the rest.

Tennis is my hobby
I like to hear them scream
I like to see the tennis ball
When it's nice and clean.

Rugby is my hobby
I like to play in teams
The rugby ball is hard to hold
When they start to scream.

Swimming is my hobby
I like to jump in the sea
When my friend comes after me
I get nice and clean.

Ryan Kearney (11)
St Patrick's Primary School, Downpatrick

Football

Liverpool, Liverpool
Stick them in a swimming pool
Take them out
Make them shout
Chelsea are so nifty
They only cost two-fifty
Terry goes to Tesco's
Where he buys his best clothes.

Johnny Collins (11)
St Patrick's Primary School, Downpatrick

Football

When the referee blows his whistle
It means I'm ready to run,
The aim of the game is win, win, win
But also have some fun.

The ball soars towards our goal,
The manager begins to shout,
'Come on boys! That's too near!
It's time that ball was out.'

All of a sudden, the ball is at my feet,
I take it around, then suddenly I'm found,
I quickly pass it to Pete.

He flicks it back,
I give it a whack,
It heads towards the goal.
Will it go in? We really want to win,
But, no! It hits the pole.

Nathan Oakes (11)
St Patrick's Primary School, Downpatrick

Soccer

The keeper's ready not to concede
Standing on his line with fear
Ready for both sides to compete

Defender stuck tight to the striker
Ready to get stuck in with slides
Instead, the striker is as fierce as a tiger

And for the attacking position
To score the screamers
They are the players to make a good decision.

Jamie Fitzpatrick (11)
St Patrick's Primary School, Downpatrick

Liverpool FC

Gerrard will never quit
Because Liverpool is his team.
He plays for his fans,
Just listen to them scream.

Riise is the champ,
He has a wicked left foot,
There's another goal,
Because he smacked it with his boot.

The final of the year,
Is just two days away,
Carragher's warming up,
To beat Milan that day.

Liverpool are ready,
Come on fans, stop frowning,
Wednesday is going to be,
Liverpool's Champions League crowning.

Ryan Vaughan (11)
St Patrick's Primary School, Downpatrick

Birthdays

Birthdays are such fun,
You get yummy food in your tum,
Screaming and shouting, jump and run,
Then we all fall on our bum.

Getting presents is the best,
But after a while we need a rest,
Tomorrow I have a maths test,
But yay for birthdays, they are still the best.

The cake is so good,
I am in a fab mood,
All the food is delicious,
The grannies try to kiss us.

Birthdays are so cool,
Way better than school.
My toy cupboard is almost full,
But what can I say, except for . . .

Birthdays rule!

Gareth Robinson (11)
St Patrick's Primary School, Downpatrick

Growing Up

As a baby you're beautiful and light,
Your skin as soft as velvet,
You hardly ever sleep well at night,
Screaming and crying instead.

As a toddler you've learnt to speak,
And now you never stop,
Off the baby food, you have many things to eat,
And playing with new found friends.

Finally a child, you go to school,
Wondering how you'll fit in,
Trying to do handwriting that's cool,
Getting shouted at by teachers for things you didn't do.

An adult you are now, getting old,
Got your license
For the road,
Getting married, happy forever.

Paul Martin (11)
St Patrick's Primary School, Downpatrick

Sunny Days

It is a sunny day
I want to go out and play
The sun beams
On my ice cream

I go and sunbathe
I see my friends and I wave
Look at that sun
When I eat my bun

I feel the sand
When I listen to the band
Forget the TV
Let's go play in the sea

We get a homework pass
Outside is so class
Forget the inside
Let's go on the water slides.

Dylan Graham (10)
St Patrick's Primary School, Downpatrick

Football

I think football is my favourite sport,
And Man United are the team that I support.
My heroes, never mind all those other teams,
Playing their matches at the theatre of dreams.

United, United, is our most popular cheer,
As the Red Devils win the League for another year.
Ronaldo runs around everywhere, just like a bit of a loony,
Then sends in a great cross, to be netted by Wayne Rooney.

Our home matches, we usually win, as a rule,
Against any other team, even Chelsea and Liverpool.
Arsenal and Spurs tried, but could not keep it up,
They couldn't even win the FA or Carling Cup.

Chelsea won them both, now claiming they had a good season,
But I really don't think so and here is my reason:
United claimed the Premiership, champions of 2007,
And all of us Red supporters think we're in Heaven.

Jonathan Deeny (11)
St Patrick's Primary School, Downpatrick

Birthdays

I like birthdays, you always have a party,
I like balloons, I like to pop them,
I like all the presents,
I like to open them, opening the boxes,
But it's a bit hard.
I like to have cake at parties,
My favourite cake is chocolate,
It is delicious.
I like to celebrate birthdays
Because you have a lot of fun
And you can play all day.

Adam Kerr
St Patrick's Primary School, Downpatrick

Liverpool

We've won it five times, more than the rest,
Because we are the best.
With Gerrard and Riise and Carragher too,
We know we will beat you.
We will win on Wednesday without a doubt,
Because Milan will be on a goal scoring drought.
Crouch is big and Bellamy is small,
Does it matter when they're so good on the ball?
Riise has a foot like a rocket,
Hopefully they won't know how to stop it.
Hopefully Kewell will be fit for the game,
Not to come off at two minutes again.
Milan are the favourites, Liverpool are not,
But who really cares when we've got the lot?

Joel McConvey (11)
St Patrick's Primary School, Downpatrick

Sport

I like sport, I like football
I like kicking, I like shooting
I like tripping people up and making them fall.

I like sport, I like swimming
I like going forwards, I like going backwards,
I like lifesaving swimming.

I like sport, I like cricket
I like batting, I like being outfield
I like putting someone out by hitting the wicket.

I like sport, I like tennis
I like winning, I don't like losing
I like acting the menace when playing tennis.

Christopher McKenna (10)
St Patrick's Primary School, Downpatrick

The Barn

In the barn birds build their nests
In the barn they lay their eggs
In the barn the owls are whistling
In the barn the mice are rustling.

This is a place I like to go
To escape from the rain or cold or snow
It's warm and safe and very big
For playing football or a game of tig.

The straw is jaggy when you sit
But soft when you fall on and nice to sniff
The bales of straw are packed so tight
You can slide and play with great delight.

The barn is full of stuff we need
To feed the cattle and sow the seed
And so it's very clear to me
The barn is just the place to be!

Michael McQuaide (11)
St Teresa's Primary School, Mountnorris

In The Spring

Spring is the time of year,
When all the children scream and cheer,
Lovely weather in the spring,
All the birds come out to sing.

Watch the bees do not sting,
When they come out in the spring,
All the trees swaying in the breeze,
The river is starting to unfreeze.

All the animals being born,
On a beautiful spring morn,
All the flowers coming out,
The life of spring is all about.

Hannah Feenan (11)
St Teresa's Primary School, Mountnorris

Rabbit

Bear asked Rabbit to come along for tea,
'No!' said Rabbit. 'You'll just eat me!'
So off went Rabbit, off he went away,
Until a croc met him that very day.
'Hello!' said the croc licking the corner of his lip,
But when he tried to catch Rabbit, all he did was slip.
Then along came a bee,
'No!' said Rabbit. 'Don't sting me!'
'No!' said the bee. 'I'm here to say,
There's a dangerous tiger coming your way.'
So off did Rabbit quickly go,
But that big old tiger did follow.
'Wait!' said the tiger. 'Something is wrong,
The rabbit I was chasing is now gone.'
The tiger was right, the rabbit did go,
To a place where no one could follow.
A place where he was free to roam,
Somewhere he called 'home sweet home'!

Anastasia Ni Riabhaigh (10)
St Teresa's Primary School, Mountnorris

Spring Is Here

Young lambs leaping and bleating,
Flowers blooming and birds cheeping.

Nests appear for the rest of the year,
Filling everyone with seasonal cheer.

Grass growing green and fast,
Farmers busy, so time flies past.

Eggs everywhere, Easter is near,
What a wonderful time of the year.

Margaret McQuaide (9)
St Teresa's Primary School, Mountnorris

Spring

Spring is all around
It is kind of like a ring

Spring is like a ring,
As we sit making daisy chains
On the gentle, swaying grass.

Spring is like a ring,
Especially when the fairies dance
Gracefully in a ring,
Round the white blossom
Of the hawthorn tree.

Spring is the time of year
When everything reawakens.

Julie McSherry (11)
St Teresa's Primary School, Mountnorris

Down By The Creek

Down by the creek,
I hear the water flow,
The trees blowing to and fro.
I feel the wind fly through my hair,
I hear the dead leaves rip and tear,
The sun shines,
It clears my mind.
I listen to the birds sing,
The flower as gentle as a bird's wing.
Look at that fish!
Here comes a rainbow, make a wish!
It's all so peaceful down by the
Creek . . .

Emma Vint (10)
St Teresa's Primary School, Mountnorris

The Milking Parlour

I like the milking parlour
Where the cows go to get milked
Gathering up the cows
From the big, grassy field.

Some cows come barging in
Some come in real slow
Some cows are patient
Some cows go moo!

The Friesian is my favourite cow,
She is fat and friendly,
She allows me to walk beside her,
Without swishing me with her tail.

I think she likes my company,
But it is hard to tell with cows,
They do not smile like people
They just look at you and stare.

When all the cows are milked,
We take them to the field,
And after milking, the parlour
Is cold, empty and quiet.

Lee Carr
St Teresa's Primary School, Mountnorris

Mrs Malone

Mrs Malone is funny and nice
Sometimes she gets angry
She gives so much like she lets us get away with anything
She wants us to have a good job
Mrs Malone knows how to teach
She gives work and sometimes we get fun things to do
Mrs Malone is really smart
Mrs Malone is one of my favourite teachers.

Ryan McSherry (8)
St Teresa's Primary School, Mountnorris

The Seaside

Feel the soft sand under your feet,
Wait until the sea and your toes meet.
The sunrays shining down on you,
The sound of children's laughter too.

The motion of the waves going in and out,
Peace and quiet, no screams or shouts.
The beautiful view of the mountains and trees,
Those trees swaying gently in the cool, calm breeze.

With the seagulls above and the people below,
Everyone's wishing they would never go.
It's getting late, the people start to leave,
No one left except the birds and me.

Niamh Kelly (10)
St Teresa's Primary School, Mountnorris

The View From My Window

I look out my window,
The trees are swaying in the gentle breeze,
While the cows in the meadow graze the fresh, green grass.

I see the chapel,
The sun reflects on the colourful, stained glass windows,
The steeple reaches up to the bright blue sky,
The quiet graves sleep in the sun.

The sheep and the lambs frolic among the daisies,
White as angels, mist on the dark mountains peeping out behind
                                                        the trees.
I feel happy and warm inside when I see the beautiful sight,
When I look out my window.

Tracey McSherry (11)
St Teresa's Primary School, Mountnorris

My Wee Sister

My wee sister is funny,
My wee sister is cool,
My wee sister can throw a tantrum.
She is only one,
Yes, one year old.
She can walk,
She can talk,
She can sing a song,
She's got short brown hair
And brown eyes too,
She's nearly three feet long.
I love my sister,
Can't you see,
She's really bright
And special to me.

Shania Ruddy (8)
St Teresa's Primary School, Mountnorris

Time Flies

The moment comes, the moment goes,
Time flies, but nobody knows,
Nobody realises it's time for home,
They're far too busy writing a poem.
They say it's for a Young Writers competition,
Rumour is, it's the latest edition,
They're scribbling furiously, ideas flowing,
Not a single soul's getting ready for going.
Again the bell rings but for the final time,
So loud, it's like a church bell's chime,
Everyone gets up, positively beaming,
They finally finished their poems and this time they weren't dreaming!

Mahnoor Tughral (11)
The Irish Society's Primary School, Coleraine

My Best Friend

You are the bestest friend that I've ever had,
More than a bit, and more than a tad,
I think you're totally cool,
Way too cool for school.

You are the bestest friend that I've ever had,
You're always good and never bad,
I wish you were my sister,
So together we could play Twister.

You are the bestest friend that I've ever had,
You're always cheerful and never sad,
You're never ever highly strung,
And in our minds we will always be young.

You are the bestest friend that I've ever had!

Danni Millar (11)
The Irish Society's Primary School, Coleraine

My Guinea Pigs

My guinea pigs have small feet,
Vegetables they love to eat.
They eat hay,
But never neigh.
They always *eek*,
As well as squeak.
My guinea pigs, I love them so,
I will never let them go.

Sarah Sim (11)
The Irish Society's Primary School, Coleraine

Sleeping In School

I am starting to drift away,
But I do not know why,
My thoughts going through the ceiling
And up into the sky.

I dream that I am flying,
High up in the air,
This is such a wonderful feeling,
With wind blowing through my hair.

When I wake up from my sleep,
I am lying on my chair,
Feeling extremely tired,
Then I become aware.

People are looking at me,
In a funny way,
Oh no! I think I slept in school!
This is not my day . . .

Hayley Gibson (11)
The Irish Society's Primary School, Coleraine

The Moon Came To My Window

The moon came up to my window last night,
While I was asleep, my eyes shut tight.
It beamed at me and its light filled the room
And it made a fairyland come out of the gloom.

My desk was made from glass and it sparkled like the sea,
The carpet looked like snow and frost, but that's between you
                                                      and me,
The door was a slab of white chocolate, the whitest you can get
And my bed was a cloud, the fluffiest I've seen yet!

Although I was still asleep and dreaming,
My eyes *weren't* shut, just wide and gleaming.
The moon opened my window and said,
'Come on, my child! *Now* get out of bed!'

I sang about dragons and elves and fairies,
I sang about castles and hobbles and dairies,
The moon took it all in and then showed me a plaque,
It said, 'That's enough, come on, jump on my back!'

We sailed through the air passing fields and rivers,
Then through the Arctic which gave me the shivers,
We flew past criminals facing certain doom,
And then we found ourselves home again, just inside my room!

The moon came up to my window last night,
When I was asleep, my eyes shut tight.
It beamed at me and I knew what it knew,
Let's just say I was having déjà vu!

Claire Cooper (11)
The Irish Society's Primary School, Coleraine

Young Writers Information

We hope you have enjoyed reading this book - and that you will continue to enjoy it in the coming years.

If you like reading and writing poetry drop us a line, or give us a call, and we'll send you a free information pack.

Alternatively if you would like to order further copies of this book or any of our other titles, then please give us a call or log onto our website at www.youngwriters.co.uk

**Young Writers Information
Remus House
Coltsfoot Drive
Peterborough
PE2 9JX**

(01733) 890066